# THE FIRST CANADIANS

## A Profile Of Canada's Native People Today

**Pauline Comeau and Aldo Santin**

James Lorimer & Company
Toronto, 1990

**Canadian Cataloguing in Publication Data**

Comeau, Pauline, 1956-

The first Canadians

ISBN 1-55028-311-1 (bound)  ISBN 1-55028-309-X (pbk.)

1. Indians of North America — Canada — Government relations — . 2. Indians of North America — Canada — Politics and government. 3. Indians of North America — Canada — Social conditions. I. Santin, Aldo, 1954- . II. Title.

E92.C6 1990    323.1'197071    C90-094003-4


James Lorimer & Company, Publishers
Egerton Ryerson Memorial Building
35 Britain Street
Toronto, Ontario M5A 1R7


Printed and bound in Canada

5 4 3 2      91 92 93 94

813990X

# Contents

# Acknowledgments

When we first sat down with the editors at the *Winnipeg Free Press* in June 1988 to discuss our next assignment, we had no idea it would soon take on a life of its own. Five months later, the *Free Press* published "Indians, Strangers in Their Own Land," a twenty-four-page supplement that explored twenty years of native issues in Canada using the plight of Manitoba's aboriginal people to highlight the problems. During the five months we spent on the project, we both interviewed dozens of people — native leaders, bureaucrats from all levels of government, social scientists, doctors, nurses, and native people from all walks of life. In the political field, we personally interviewed federal Indian Affairs Minister Bill McKnight; Liberal MP Keith Penner, who headed a committee investigating native self-government; Manitoba's Premier Gary Filmon and Northern Affairs Minister James Downey. We also reviewed twenty years of documents, everything from government annual reports to academic journals; and compiled data based on the information found there. We were also able to obtain hundreds of pages of information, particularly on the events surrounding the 1969 White Paper, through the federal Freedom of Information Act.

But at the end of the project, we found ourselves with many loose ends. Time restraints and space restrictions had forced us to leave much of the original material on the cutting-room floor or completely untouched. And so, the idea for the book was born. In these pages, we take the original twenty-year focus beyond Manitoba's borders and examine many of the same issues on a national scale. To prepare for the book, we read more scholarly accounts, government reviews, conducted dozens of additional interviews with national spokespeople and government and native representatives from a variety of regions. We also applied for more information through the Freedom of Information Act. Included in this second round were personal interviews with some of the original players who were front and centre in 1969.

We are deeply grateful to all of those who gave so freely of their time and energy to pass on their personal experiences and knowledge of native issues during the two years it took to put this project together.

A special note of thanks must also be extended to our employer the *Winnipeg Free Press* for first introducing us to the subject of the plight of native Canadians and then for allowing us ready access to research material first obtained for the newspaper. We would like to specifically thank Wayne Hanna and Harold Cardinal for their time.

We are also grateful for the patience and assistance of copyeditor Linda Biesenthal and editor at James Lorimer & Company Virginia Smith, particularly for their stubborn refusal to give up on us.

Aldo wishes to thank his wife, Pamela Pyke, for her patience and support. Both Pauline and Aldo would also like to thank all their friends and colleagues, especially Dan Lett, for the much-needed support and humour they provided during the past two years, and particularly during the dark days.

Pauline Comeau
Aldo Santin
June 1990

# Introduction

It is 1989, and a senior Indian Affairs bureaucrat with more than a decade of experience stares out the eleventh-storey window of his office tower at the vast prairie and waves his arm in a gesture aimed at the public below. "What are you going to do with this information?" he asks a reporter who has arrived to cart away several boxes of data. "They don't give a damn about [Indians] you know. They couldn't care less."

Several months later, Nona Pariseau, a curious and opinionated Grade 11 student who has recently moved to the West from Halifax, approaches the authors while she is doing research for a history class. She is researching modern native history and has come armed with a question: "What is it that these Indian people want, anyway?" Speaking in tones edged with anger and frustration, she decries what she sees as native demands to return to the time of the buffalo hunt and the teepee while the rest of the world moves forward. "I never saw an Indian until I came to Winnipeg," she admits with a tinge of amazement. "I never knew they were here, in this country first."

These anecdotes reflect the extremes across Canada when it comes to opinions about this country's original residents. Anyone seeking simple answers to explain the lack of progress and on-going suffering of Canada's native people will be frustrated. There is no one enemy, no single event that will explain it all. There is, however, one factor that has shadowed the native experience throughout history and that is racism. Over the past twenty years, international human rights groups, including the United Nations, have criticized Canada for its inadequate and often discriminatory native policies. In 1989, the Canadian Human Rights Commission called the treatment of the country's aboriginal people a national tragedy.

*The First Canadians* is an attempt to explore the gains made by aboriginal people during the past twenty years, as well as the government responses to their demands for greater control of their own lives.

The federal government has spent more than $26 billion during the past twenty years providing services and programs to Indians across Canada, most of whom live in conditions that other Canadians imagine only exist in the Third World. And what is the result of all this spending?

Native Canadians die, on average, ten years sooner than other Canadians, a discrepancy that has not improved even marginally in twenty years. They are barely better educated today than they were two decades ago. They are jailed at rates that far exceed what their numbers would indicate is possible, and some experts estimate that a native Canadian is three times more likely to land in a jail cell than in a high school graduating class. And they destroy themselves at a phenomenal rate, through violence, accidents, and by choosing suicide as a way out of their misery. As one western newspaper columnist noted in a story on a young native boy's suicide: "We used to hang them. Now they hang themselves."

But it was not always this way. Long before the white settlers came, Canada's aboriginal people had created a co-operative social structure, complete with a hierarchy of political power and a fully functioning justice system. All that changed when the new settlers arrived and set about taming the "savages." Despite the insistence of a few officials that only the best of intentions motivated the newcomers, the reality was that the overwhelming arrogance of the white settlers led them to reject everything native. Laws were passed to stop Indian ceremonies. Children were taken from parents and placed in schools where their languages and culture were erased.

More than 200 years after the first arrival of white society, and without losing any of the arrogance of their predecessors, white officials announced a solution to this national tragedy. In 1969, the newly elected Liberal majority under the charismatic

Pierre Trudeau attempted for the first time to establish a national strategy that would solve the problems plaguing native Canadians once and for all. In the glow of this "Just Society" came the now infamous White Paper, a plan that the federal bureaucrats believed would lead the poverty-stricken native people to the promised land of white society. The new policy was one of equality with all Canadians through assimilation. Both the special status conferred on Canada's Indian people by the Indian Act and the separate federal department overseeing the administration of their welfare would be eliminated. The provincial governments would assume the burden of financial responsibility of native services, reserves would disappear, and Indians would eventually become an accepted part of the Canadian mosaic, no longer the victims of discrimination.

Native leaders were furious. Besides the naive assumption that something as deeply rooted as racism could be wiped out by decree, the document was proof that Ottawa had failed to understand their message. What they wanted was the right to live their lives without the hand of Ottawa meddling in their affairs at every turn. In response to the White Paper, Indian people began a year of intense and unprecedented united opposition. In 1970, feeling the weight of growing public opposition, Ottawa officially withdrew the White Paper and, at least publicly, declared that the goal now was a search for a new solution.

Failure to find the new solution has left the country without a national agenda on native issues. In its place there have been a thousand small skirmishes waged almost every day on every conceivable front — from the local band chiefs staking out areas of independence, to the clash of visions between cynical civil servants and idealistic politicians, to battles in the national and international courts. *The First Canadians* takes a closer look at some of these skirmishes to reveal just how complex and frustrating the problems are.

An examination of the intrigue surrounding the White Paper reveals a bureaucracy that was at its best naive and, at its worst, duplicitous. There is clear evidence twenty years later that, despite government rhetoric about accommodating the demands of native people, the White Paper's assumptions about the proper course for native affairs continue to determine many federal decisions.

The struggle for Indian self-government has been plagued with its own problems, not the least of which has been a lack of know-how on the part of native leaders and a small, often fractured aboriginal population that has frequently found it difficult to put aside its own differences in fights against the common enemy. The struggle is exacerbated by the failure on both sides to reach an acceptable definition of self-government. The ultimate native vision sees the country dotted with hundreds of First Nations, today's reserves, that are given the status of a third level of government, equal in stature to the provinces. Instead, Ottawa has offered Indian people bits and pieces of control, some of it in response to native demands, but more of it as a way of satisfying its own agenda of reducing its financial and constitutional responsibilities while ensuring that the division of power remains intact.

In *The First Canadians* Indian leaders describe their own gains and losses in the fields of economic development, health care, education, child welfare, and justice. These policy areas have become the working laboratories for self-government, providing proof that they are capable of handling their own affairs and improving the lives of their people without the record of tragedy produced by Ottawa. Leading the struggle are the native men and women and their political organizations which have evolved over the past twenty years from small, single-issue lobby groups to complex, multifaceted machines led by individuals capable of meeting their opponents head to head in any battle.

"Everyone is listening now," says Judge Murray Sinclair, an Ojibway Indian and the associate chief judge of the Manitoba provincial court. What they are hearing is the message the native elders have passed down through the generations. And, even if we miss this chance as Canadians to hear it yet again, history has shown that the native people will not give up. As one native leader said: "We can't sit back for a minute.... If we quit, what will happen to our children?"

# 1

# The White Paper

When the Canadian government is preparing to take a new public stand on an issue, it releases its "intended" policy direction in a document called a White Paper. After debate and final shaping, these documents are filed away under their official titles in the national archives and then usually forgotten.

But for Canada's aboriginal people, there is one such document that refuses to disappear among the volumes of other policy papers gathering dust in Ottawa — "The Statement of the Government of Canada on Indian Policy." Its official title may be forgotten but the document lives on in the collective modern Indian psyche. It is simply called the White Paper, three words that inevitably trigger heated discussion, debate, and anger twenty years after its creation.

It was on June 25, 1969, that Indian Affairs Minister Jean Chrétien stood before the first session of the 28th Parliament to read the thirteen-page White Paper. Watching from the visitors' gallery were Indian leaders who had been called to Ottawa to be on hand for the historic occasion.

Twenty years later, David Courchene, Sr., leader of the Manitoba Indian Brotherhood at the time, still remembers the excitement of that day. "We didn't know anything about the 1969 White Paper until we were called to Ottawa by the minister," says Courchene, sitting in his log home on the Fort Alexander Indian Reserve, about an hour's drive north of

Winnipeg. "All the national organizations, the General Assembly Group it was called then, were there. There must have been hundreds of us in Ottawa that day." He recalls that the leaders met briefly with the minister before being seated in the gallery and introduced to the House. Following a short debate, all eyes turned to Chrétien as he began reading the White Paper. And for the first time, the assembled native leaders heard that the government's new policy called for, among other things, the abolition of the Indian Act and all special status for Canada's 265,000 registered Indians. "We couldn't believe it," says Courchene, his voice rising in memory of the shock he felt. "He was transferring everything to the provinces and washing his hands of the Indians. And he said he had consulted with us. That was bullshit."

Within hours of the announcement, it became clear that something was seriously wrong. Stunned by what they had heard, the Indian leaders met the next day and released a letter denouncing the government's intentions. "One hundred years from now our grandchildren will reap the consequences of the actions we take in the next few days — just as we are the inheritors of a legacy brought about by the actions of our forefathers," stated the six-page response signed by eight chiefs and co-chairs of the National Indian Brotherhood. "The Minister has made a mistake. We appreciate the Minister's concern and do not question his good will."

According to Courchene, the native leaders, who were often criticized for internal bickering and their failure to reach a consensus, had no trouble speaking as one that day. "We were being pushed like the Métis people into the hands of the provinces who didn't look after the Métis. So how could they look after the Indian?" And Chrétien's reaction to the chorus of protest? "He couldn't believe us," recalls Courchene. "Just as we couldn't believe him."

There were six basic points in the new policy. The Indian Act, drawn up in 1876 to formalize the relationship between the Crown and native people, would be repealed leaving Indians with no different status than any other Canadian. Other federal departments and levels of government, particularly the provinces, would provide services for Indians in the same way they provided services for other Canadian residents — as a result, the Department of Indian Affairs would be dismantled within five years. Indians would be given control of Indian lands. Everyone in Canada would recognize the "unique contribution" that native people had made to the country. Those furthest behind would be helped the most. And finally, "lawful obligations" would be met. An Indian Policy Group, later called the Implementation Group, and still later, the Consultation and Negotiations Group, was named to carry out the government's plan.

The most contentious piece of the policy was, of course, the main item. According to the authors of the paper, the Indian Act was the key reason for discrimination against Indian people. The special status conferred on them by the act, along with the separate government department established to care for their needs, was deemed to be the major stumbling block to native progress. Remove that distinction, the bureaucrats reasoned, and the rest would almost take care of itself. "Special treatment has made of the Indians a community disadvantaged and apart," announced the paper's prologue. "The policy of separation has become a burden. This 'differentness' must not be enshrined in legislation," Chrétien would tell the country later.

The government jumped right in and sent out bureaucratic troops to sell this ideal of assimilation. Negative reaction was met with typical bureaucratic self-confidence, reflecting the government's firm belief that Indians were simply overreacting because of their historic distrust of anything to do with government, and that things would calm down once the Indians had time to digest and accept the policy's proposals. It would all prove to be a fateful miscalculation for the survival of the White Paper.

Instead of disappearing, the protests grew. Provincial leaders, who were being asked to accept responsibility for native people and the programs supporting them, eventually joined Indian leaders in denouncing the White Paper. "We do not want the problem thrown on our hands," said Saskatchewan

Premier Ross Thatcher several months after the paper's release. Other provincial leaders insisted that they had no wish to ignore their responsibilities to Indians as residents of their provinces, but that nothing could be done until the Indians and the federal government had settled their differences and until Ottawa was ready to reimburse the provinces for the extra financial burden.

According to internal documents, newspapers across the country were closely monitored by the government as a measuring stick of public opinion. And reaction was strong. There were the usual articles for and against the policy. And then there was a series of stinging attacks delivered by editorial writers and columnists. In a July edition of the Vancouver *Province*, Eric Nicol wrote: "The Indian Affairs minister has offered the Indians equality with the white man. Naturally, the Indians rejected what they saw as a retrograde step — like offering the snow goose equality with Donald Duck." Another article stated: "As all species reproduce only their own kind and no other, thus the new policy ... is a baby white elephant of the same breed as its parent, the Department of Indian Affairs."

Included in the deluge of letters that arrived in Chrétien's office were dozens written by Indians. "We got to keep our special rights," wrote one. "Take them away and you leave us nothing, you, and your just society. One last thing. We are Canadians by birth. We don't need a law passed to change us into Canadians. So I suppose the law is to tell the white man what we are. And if it takes a law to do that, God help us."

## A New Response

The bureaucracy changed its tactic. Within weeks of the first criticism, a new response from Ottawa emerged. Chrétien and his staff insisted that the problem was that people were confused about what the policy actually meant. "I believe you have misunderstood the intent of my policy proposals" repeated the thousands of form letters that poured out of Ottawa. Chrétien began touring the country, and eventually developed a speech that focused on "what this policy does *not* say" in an attempt to clear up the perceived confusion and the growing protest.

"This statement is *not* a final policy," said Chrétien in a speech in Regina in October 1969. He was attempting to quell the anger over an Indian policy that lacked any Indian input. "This statement does *not* propose or suggest that Indian reserves be abolished. The statement does *not* propose that provincial governments should take over responsibility for Indian land." And on and on he went, responding to the growing fears of native people across Canada.

Another major point of contention was the question of whether or not the new policy was a fait accompli. The Indian Policy Group's title of Implementation Group was dropped because it sounded as if there was no room for Indian input. But the name change appeared to be only cosmetic to native leaders. Ironically, the government's repeated attempts to reassure Indians that they were to be active participants in the new policy gave even more credence to their distrust, because what Ottawa was saying was that Indians would be asked to help advance and implement the policy.

"The proposals contained in the policy paper are subject to consultation with Indian people," Chrétien wrote in September 1969 in a letter to the National Indian Brotherhood. "Indians will be offered every opportunity to participate in further development of the proposed policy and in bringing it into effect." A month earlier, an Indian Affairs Department deputy minister, John A. McDonald, had sent a letter to his staff which stated that the White Paper "sets forth not only certain principles, which are incontrovertible, but also a number of proposals or actions which are subject to modification in substance in the light of alternatives that may be suggested by the Indian people...."

The New Democratic Party and a few other lone voices across the country joined the native protest. As they pointed out, the only thing Indians were being asked to "consult" on was *how* to implement the policy, not on whether the policy itself should exist at all.

And Indians claimed that, despite Chrétien's insistence about what the paper actually said, the end result of implementing the policy would be assimilation, or "cultural genocide," as the National Indian Brotherhood called it. In turn, this would lead to the eventual loss of control over their lands. For Indians in 1969, as now, any perceived threat to their control over land was cause for grave concern because dreams of Indian sovereignty and power are rooted in their rights to their land.

Indians were also angry that the policy announcement came only a few weeks after a series of nineteen meetings between Indian leaders and government officials had ended. To the Indians, the consultation process they had been involved in for nine months had suddenly been aborted. None of their concerns, particularly an emphasis on how to change the Indian Act for the better, was addressed in the policy. "They spoke with a forked tongue," says Harold Cardinal, the young and often rebellious leader of the Indian Association of Alberta in 1969. According to Cardinal, the meetings with the government had concentrated on ways to change the Indian Act for the benefit of Indians, something that led Indian leaders to believe that there would still be an Indian Act. "And all the while, the internal process was that, if they were going to pursue their policy of equality, then there was no need for special legislation."

A speech by Chrétien early in these consultation talks adds weight to Indian claims that they were led astray. "As a result of the consultations we have had with them until now," Chrétien told the House in late 1968, "it is obvious that under the terms of the new Indian Act, we will give them more authority on both the reserve and band levels in order to enable them to control their own destiny...."

Twenty years later, Cardinal explains why, even if different messages were given just prior to the White Paper's release, native leaders were so unprepared for the affront. Since the passing of the Indian Act in 1876, Indians in Canada have been waging a battle to gain some recognition of what they see as their rights to exist as a separate political entity. Their vision of self-government was understood by Indian elders and their students, but by virtually no one else in the country. Cardinal points to several key events that led to the slow emergence of a clearer, more publicly defined vision. First were changes in the Indian Act during the 1950s that gave Indians the legal right to organize. That was followed by the right to vote in federal elections, granted in 1960.

With those two events behind them, Cardinal says, Indians were working in the late 1960s under the assumption that the question of their legal status had been all but resolved, if not in any concrete, legal sense, at least as an understood and accepted long-term goal. Thus Indian leaders had turned their attention elsewhere. In 1969 when the White Paper came out, they were busy with other things — including the building of their own political organizations, which was the next stage in gaining recognition of their place as part of the political equation in Canada. "There was this notion that since this first step was achieved in the native political agenda [voting rights] in terms of having the Indian person recognized, that the next step would be to have the Canadian nation state recognize the collective entities that made it possible for Canada to be what it is today. That's our Indian nations," says Cardinal.

Instead, the White Paper announced that the government intended to move in an entirely new direction, one that would eliminate separateness and make Indians equal to all other Canadians with no more right to self-government initiatives than anyone else. "They didn't want to recognize us as Indians, and I think that was why our reaction was so strong," Cardinal says. "We thought at least that basic step had been passed in 1960."

Over the years, historians, bureaucrats, and some Indian leaders have pointed to the White Paper as a major catalyst for a renewed vigour among the Indian leadership. Some even point to it as a major contributor to the advances Canada's aboriginal people have realized since 1969. "For the first time, the real problems of Indian people, and the basic issues at stake were clearly revealed, considered and argued over," stated one Indian Affairs civil servant in a letter dated one year after the paper's release. "The old paternalism and tolerance of legislative discrimination has gone forever," maintained another. "And so has the apathy of the Indian people so evident three or four years ago. There is, indeed, a new spirit abroad."

"I think the White Paper was one of the most destructive documents to ever come out," says Cardinal. "I think there was a political revival taking place right across the country among various Indian people. It was fueled by the kinds of rights movements that were occurring in the U.S.... There was a basic yearning for democracy, and the government of the day had an opportunity to join forces with that. I think the White Paper sidetracked the kind of developments that had to go on." But, according to Cardinal, the policy did accomplish one thing: it forced Indian leaders to regroup and work on their counterattack. Cardinal says that the conflict and point-counterpoint established then still continues, but now the tide has turned: now it is native people who have a very clear sense of what they want, and it is the federal government that is struggling for some sense of direction.

It took more than a year for native leaders to respond officially to the White Paper. They delivered two major responses, consisting of hundreds of pages detailing the direction Indians felt they should be taking. Cardinal's "Citizens Plus," often referred to as the "Red Paper," dealt with land claims and economic policies. It was presented to Prime Minister Pierre Trudeau on July 4, 1970. David Courchene's report from Manitoba, *Wahbung, Our Tomorrow*, was released in October 1971. It covered a wide spectrum of native issues in detail, everything from land claims and culture to housing, education, and on-reserve government.

While the Indians were preparing their responses, Chrétien found himself at centre stage facing an increasingly hostile and emotional Indian population. In Alberta, bands refused to meet with him, saying they could not guarantee his safety. A memo to the government written by an Indian Affairs superintendent on a Six Nations Indian Reserve described a meeting this way: "Councillor Mrs. Rena Hill almost broke down in the middle of her talk. She asked the Indians to unite and avoid violence, reminding them that the Six Nations were dignified, and proud Indians." A petition was sent to the Queen, asking her to intervene because Canada planned to unilaterally remove rights that had been bestowed on Indians by the Crown. In Winnipeg, Indians burned the document in front of Chrétien.

It was in the midst of all this that Prime Minister Trudeau authored the now famous statement that aboriginal rights could not be recognized "because no society can be built on historical 'might have beens,'" as well as other less-than-sympathetic words of wisdom. In an television interview in March 1970, Trudeau left little doubt about how he felt history would unfold if Indians rejected the White Paper. "We are not forcing anyone to do anything," he said. "We'll keep them in the ghetto as long as they want." The words reflected Trudeau's belief at the time that Indians had no claims to sovereignty. He expanded on these points and offered several rather prophetic warnings in a letter to Chrétien in November 1969.

"All the reports I have indicate you have the situation well in hand," wrote Trudeau, adding that he felt Indian communities simply needed time to absorb the information. Although he suggested a flexible approach with the Indians, he felt a more forceful one was needed with the provinces. Trudeau wanted to move quickly before provincial leaders united behind Alberta and British Columbia. These western provinces have historically led the fight against changes to give native people more rights, and they were sure to reject calls for more provincial responsibility in this area. "A common front of the provincial governments and the Indian communities would make negotiations very difficult," wrote Trudeau. "In the same manner, the participation of the Indians in the negotiating meetings of the two levels of government concerning the transfer of services, seems to me to pose serious difficulties. If the Indians are present in a capacity other than as technical advisors of their respective governments, they would, by that fact, acquire a status at par with the status of the government." (This is, of course, the very status native leaders have sought for more than a century.)

Trudeau also suggested in the letter that the government's discussions should include not only registered Indians but all of Canada's aboriginal people, including the Métis. For years, Indian leaders have accused governments of attempting to

weaken the native advances since the White Paper by purpose-
fully undermining the growing strength and visibility of Indian
groups simply by drawing all aboriginal people into the debate.
However, there is no hint in the Trudeau letter that his thoughts
about including the Métis had any diabolical root or intent.
Coming from a point of view that gave no credibility to the
notion of a separate native level of government, Trudeau was
left with plenty of room to ponder the larger philosophical
question of just who was and who was not an Indian. "Those
not registered are as numerous as those registered; they are
living, to a large extent, in the same localities, share the same
set of values and are suffering from the same discrimination on
the part of white society."

After more than a year of fighting, Chrétien had no choice
but to admit that the protests ran deeper than misunderstanding
and simple overreaction. He also had to admit that the protests
were not going to disappear. The White Paper was officially
withdrawn in the spring of 1970.

Indian leaders take some pride in the fact that their protest,
as unsophisticated as it was at the time, was nevertheless effective. "We stopped it anyway," says David Courchene, with
more than a hint of resignation. "It [the White Paper] was not
made into national policy." However, Cardinal and Courchene
believe that, overall, their battle had little effect on the endless
attempts by government to ignore their long-term and short-
term aims and that, in the end, the government's plan for them
simply went underground. "If we had been successful, we
would have been involved in negotiations through the Prime
Minister's Office on the question of disbanding Indian Affairs...." said Cardinal in 1989. "If we had been successful, we
would have independently funded political organizations....
We would have Indian control over a university and technical
training programs to tackle the development program. On most
fronts we lost bad. I think we failed. And in some ways, it is
really tragic."

# Demise of the White Paper

A behind-the-scenes examination indicates that, along with the Indian protest, there were numerous other elements in the mix that contributed to the official demise of the White Paper's Indian policy. First, the paper showed a profound naiveté not only about the roots of the Indian problem, but also about how the world would unfold once the policy went into effect. Not only would the massive Indian Affairs Department fade away within five years (a time period many laughed at), but the deep-rooted socioeconomic problems facing Canada's aboriginal people would be solved within no more than thirty years.

In February 1970, Chrétien wrote to Manitoba Premier Edward Schreyer outlining the government's view on how the provincial takeover of Indian responsibility would unfold. According to its basic scheme, Ottawa would sign an agreement with the province guaranteeing funding at current levels for Indian services. This would be followed by a ten-year period in which the money would increase in step with the increase in native population and need. Another ten-year period would follow, in which the financial pay-out would be constant, and then there would be another ten years when the payments would be phased out. "Over the entire period of the agreement, we see the Indian people improving their economic position and their earning ability and, as a consequence, producing a substantially greater proportion of provincial tax revenues," wrote Chrétien.

Is it any wonder the provinces backed off? Chrétien admitted in the letter that Ottawa believed Indians would continue to migrate to urban centres, which would result in the eventual demise of remote reserves. Not only have reserves failed to disappear in the past twenty years, but a massive infusion of money has failed to improve the economic status of Indians. They are not even close to the point where the provinces could consider them a tax bonus instead of a burden.

On top of what might have been just some very bad arithmetic on Chrétien's part was another major flaw in the process — the total lack of a game plan. Perhaps this problem was another reason why Ottawa failed to move ahead with the policy it had so much confidence in. Internal documents show that after the general policy outline was released, there were few specifics (beyond the announcement that a lands claim commissioner would be appointed) and absolutely no mechanism ready to carry out the necessary restructuring of government departments and service delivery across the country. In the weeks and months following the policy's release, bureaucrats complained to head office about everything: there were not enough copies of the policy and none available in aboriginal languages; the document had been released during fishing season when many Indians were in the bush; there was no blueprint outlining exactly what was to happen next.

Indian Affairs employees were informed their department would disappear in five years, and then were given no guidelines on how to proceed or on what to do. With no direction, those in the field could not answer the simplest questions and often gave conflicting responses. When someone accused the government of stealing a U.S. policy, which had failed during the 1950s, the government had no response. (In fact, documents show it was totally unaware of the U.S. policy and only researched the whole issue six months after academics wrote letters to the editor which pointed out the similarities.) And yet another complaint: "We do not now have the precise information we need respecting the position of Indians in each province vis-à-vis the extent to which they require services and the degree to which they contribute to the provincial economy and treasury," wrote one bureaucrat in October 1969, adding that the cost/benefit information would have major bearings on discussions with provincial leaders.

By the spring of 1970, Ottawa had coined a new phrase: "A search for common ground." The government conceded that what was needed was an entirely new approach, one that would include Indian leaders right from the beginning. These were certainly conciliatory words but little seems to have come of them.

With growing frequency, Indian leaders and scholars have insisted over the past two decades that the White Paper simply went underground, and continues to be the main driving force behind the government's native policy. One piece of evidence to support this notion is the fact that, with no official agreement on the table, the provinces have slowly acquired a greater degree of responsibility over the administration of Indian Affairs dollars. Documents show that, between 1982 and 1987, Indians and provincial governments have shared almost equally the spoils of what the federal government has relinquished. The provincial share almost tripled during that period; in 1988 the provinces controlled 13 per cent of the federal government's $1.7 billion Indian Affairs budget, for a total of $219 million.

There is more evidence from internal documents written immediately after the White Paper was officially withdrawn. In a paper dated April 1, 1970, Indian Affairs deputy minister David Munro pieced together for a newly appointed bureaucrat the history of the White Paper in which he advanced several notions about how the government should proceed. Not once in the paper did he ever suggest that the government's basic premise was flawed. Despite all the debates and protests, Munro still believed that Indian leaders had simply "failed or declined to understand the policy proposals." He went on to outline "obstacles to further progress" as well as "tactical" changes: "We can still believe with just as much strength and sincerity that the policies we propose are the right ones, and we should inform and persuade the Indian people to that end with the greatest effort we can muster. If our concepts and proposals are indeed correct, they will be accepted by all but a few once they are understood."

Munro was convinced that each element in the policy, even the devolution of Indian Affairs, would occur. "But the pace of acceptance will vary in accordance with the degree of acculturation and sophistication of the groups of people concerned." And on the issue of the removal of special status, he wrote: it "must be relegated far into the future.... If pressed on the question, we should respond to the effect that the government considers the elimination of special status to be ultimately desirable but it is not about to force the issue now." He suggested that the government make two "concessions," as he called them. First, the government should make a public statement about the need to discuss aboriginal rights. Second, it should return to a pre-White Paper document which had been collecting dust.

In the two years before Indian leaders and government representatives began the series of nineteen meetings which preceded the release of the White Paper, Indian Affairs decision-makers were digesting data contained in a document prepared for Indian Affairs by Harry B. Hawthorn. *A Survey of Contemporary Indians of Canada* was described by Indian Affairs bureaucrats as a "thorough and scholarly" document offering "sound research and ... practical recommendations." The report concluded that notions of integration and assimilation were not reasonable avenues to pursue for Canada's aboriginal people and called instead for an all-out effort that focused on education, programs that would increase Indians' income potential, and improved health care. As well, the report said, Indians should be regarded as "citizens-plus," a group with rights beyond other Canadians because they were the country's original residents. Although Hawthorn's paper had been set aside in early 1969 for the new policy focusing on the elimination of separate status, in 1970 Munro suggested that, "for an interim period," the government partially return to Hawthorn's recommendations, particularly the spending of major funds on education, health, and economic development. Considering Munro's other views in the memo, it is likely he thought these expenditures would only be required until Indian leaders accepted the White Paper policy or until, as Hawthorn's report predicted, most Indians had moved off reserves into urban settings and had become, by default, the responsibility of others.

## Virtually No Success
Since then, the Department of Indian Affairs and Northern Development alone has spent more than $16 billion in an attempt to help Indians out of their socioeconomic gutter — with virtually no success. Some of those expenditures can be linked to the White Paper, such as a general $50-million

program for economic development initiatives and funds to help Indian organizations. The latter may be a decision the government will long regret. Initially, the idea was to strengthen those organizations so their leaders could become the chief negotiators with Ottawa to carry out the White Paper's proposals. Instead, the money has helped these native groups take their battle for rights into other forums.

The withdrawal of the White Paper from the political arena effectively left the issue of aboriginal rights without an over-riding political scheme or direction. As a result, the battle to define aboriginal rights, at least at the bureaucratic level, has been waged almost on a policy-by-policy and department-by-department basis and has moved to a number of different forums, some inside and some outside the political agenda.

On the federal level, the search for new ground initially led to what is popularly known as devolution. This notion took root during the 1970s and was the government's response to native calls for self-determination. Devolution involves the govern-ment handing over to Indians, in various stages, control over certain administrative services. Ottawa, however, would main-tain the role of overseer and overall policy director and would control, for all intents and purposes, the purse strings.

On the native front, things have gone in a different direction within this political vacuum. From the scattered native or-ganizations with undefined and general goals in 1969, Indian groups have emerged in the 1980s with a much clearer notion of self-government. They work now on a variety of fronts, from the political to the legal, to guarantee its survival. For the most part, they reject devolution as only a half-measure.

Many of the struggles along the way have left Canada's aboriginal people frustrated and angry over what they see as a lack of progress. Others, however, have offered a glimmer of hope, particularly in the courtroom. In 1973, Trudeau found himself rethinking his "might-have-been" ideas after the Nish-ga band of British Columbia managed to take the first com-prehensive land claim before the Supreme Court of Canada. Six of the seven judges ruled that native people had a right to the land they occupied. Specifically on the Nishga case, three judges ruled that the band's claim to land in northern British Columbia still existed, three said it did not, and the seventh gave no opinion, dismissing the case on a technicality.

Although the case was not an out-and-out victory, it did mean that Indian land claims could not be easily dismissed again. Harold Cardinal says the ruling made Trudeau, an expert in constitutional law, and his Liberal party rethink their approach: "Trudeau took a step back and said, 'Well, I guess we were wrong, there's something in there.' At least there was a willingness to deal with that. On that basis, I think the federal government initiated discussions, some of which are still going on today."

In comparison, Cardinal talks about another court victory. The issue of the federal government's historic responsibility as trustee of Indian rights and claims on behalf of the Crown was the essential ingredient in the 1985 Musquiam case. In a decision that Indian leaders believe could have far-reaching implications, the Supreme Court of Canada awarded the Musquiam band $10 million to cover its estimated losses in potential development of a golf course which the federal government, in its role as trustee, had overseen since a deal was struck in the 1950s. The court rejected the government's position that its role as trustee fell within the political venue and could not be subjected to court action.

"In a number of very fundamental policy points of view, the Supreme Court sustained, adopted, accepted, or ratified the fundamental positions that our people have been taking," Cardinal explains. "But the federal government has adopted what I call a trench warfare mentality, or a containment policy," he says about the response of the Conservative government under Brian Mulroney. "They have, I think somewhat successfully, succeeded in burying that court decision." Cardinal believes the government's aim is to wait for more court tests on the trust question. "They have been found guilty in not fulfilling their trust responsibility in the way land disposal was handled. So they said, 'Maybe in the context. But we will wait and see more tests.'"

A major area of frustration, and one that has native people looking more and more often to the courts and elsewhere for satisfaction, has been the aboriginal struggle to win legal guarantees or recognition of their rights throughout the constitutional debate of the 1980s. After last-minute scrambling in 1981, they were left with this catch-all provision in the Charter of Rights and Freedoms: "That existing aboriginal and treaty rights would be recognized." Attempts to strengthen that provision during a series of constitutional conferences ended in failure in 1987. Key provincial leaders joined with their Ottawa counterparts to argue that the concepts of "self-government were too vague to be approved."

Weeks later, Mulroney and the provincial premiers emerged from Meech Lake to announce that they had struck an agreement which would bring the province of Quebec, also left out of the Constitution in 1981, into the federation by recognizing it as a "distinct society." The irony of the government's failure to explain what that phrase meant in concrete terms, and the notion that it could all be worked out later between the two "founding nations of Canada, the English and the French," was not lost on Canada's original people. Here again was more evidence that they were not an integral part of the collective Canadian psyche. In 1990, native issues returned to haunt the First ministers during the very final stages of the Meech approval process.

Posturings on the political front throughout the 1980s continued their one-step-forward, one-step-back pattern as Canada's native people struggled to wrestle some control from Ottawa. A 1983 parliamentary committee, chaired by Liberal MP Keith Penner, recommended after months of study and travel across the country that Indian First Nations be recognized and treated as equals with the provinces. Two years later, under a Conservative government, the Nielsen Task Force report on government spending suggested — as the White Paper had in 1969 — that responsibility for Indians be shifted to the provinces as a cost-saving measure, a recommendation that gave native leaders yet more ammunition for their claim that the White Paper and the government's hopes for assimilation were alive and well in Ottawa.

However, Canada's native leaders have no intention of leaving the battle zone now that they have gained a measure of success on some fronts. They continue to fight the government's move towards assimilation as hard as ever. David Courchene, Sr., and others believe that their final battles eventually will be waged on the international stage. "I believe that the Canadian Indian and the American Indian can develop a court case against the governments of Canada and the United States to go before an international court or tribunal," he says, adding that the exact forum has yet to be decided. Once a decision against the government is reached, then a deal can be negotiated.

act, it has been in the international human rights arena that native people have found some renewed hope in the past decade. Indian leaders in 1969 gained some early experiences in the international forum. In response to the White Paper, a delegation travelled to London to ask the Queen to intervene on their behalf. Twenty years later, their approach has become far more sophisticated.

In October 1980, in the midst of the constitutional debate, the National Indian Brotherhood opened an office in London with the hopes of lobbying British MPs to block the resolution until it included aboriginal rights. In the same month, an international tribunal on human rights held in Amsterdam and sponsored by the Bertrand Russell Peace Foundation issued a ruling against the Canadian government, declaring it guilty of "ethnocide" because of its treatment of native people.

The Lubicon Indian Band of Alberta has become one of the better-known bands in the nation because of its protracted and well-publicized lobby campaigns aimed at bringing public attention to a fifty-year-old land claim dispute with Alberta and Ottawa. The band's most successful manoeuvres came in 1988 when it gained international attention by staging a very vocal boycott of a native art exhibit held during the Calgary Winter Olympics. The international media, looking for a different angle on the Olympics and on Canada, wrote volumes on the long and bitter battle.

Talks between the band, led by Chief Bernard Ominayak, and the federal government broke off in February 1988 after the band rejected a package involving a 245-square-kilometre reserve and $45 million for housing, community facilities, and economic development. The band is seeking up to $200 million in compensation for lost oil and gas revenues. In November 1989, the band renewed its publicity campaign. In a letter sent electronically to the prime minister, Ominayak delivered notice that the nationally owned oil company, Petro-Canada, had thirty days to obtain band permits and begin paying royalties for using disputed land about 500 kilometres northwest of Edmonton. Failure to comply would be met with eviction, the letter warned. One month later, band members began patrolling the land and threatened to dismantle the oil wells. Petro-Canada shut down two wells as a precautionary measure. The band declared the exercise a success despite the fact that the government says it has no intention of budging on its "fair offer." Ominayak is also not moving and the stalemate continues with expectations that the band has more cards up its sleeve.

Fear of embarrassment on the international stage may be forcing the government's hand. There is a new note being sounded across the country. Scholars and politicians, editorial writers and some Indian leaders are calling for a royal commission to study and settle the native issue once and for all. They are all demanding that the government come to terms with the problems facing Canada's original people by working out with native leaders a distinct course for native self-government.

# 2

# Reserves

Pukatawagan is a Cree community sitting along the north shore of the Churchill River in northern Manitoba, 750 kilometres northwest of Winnipeg and a short distance from the Saskatchewan border. Thirteen hundred people call it home. The Department of Indian Affairs lists the band's official name as Mathias Colomb, after the chief who settled the band in its present location at the turn of the century. The Cree call themselves Missinippi Ethiniwak or the Churchill River people. The band is one of 596 bands across Canada and typical of the 125 bands found in the northern extremes of the country, located so far from the rest of the world that no one has bothered to build a road to get there. The only way in or out is by air. The community is bordered by dense bush and the wide river. The streets are dirt roads. There are a few trucks and vans on the reserve, but there is nowhere for them to go. The road ends at the airstrip and a rail line. It is a quiet community, but not a stagnant one. In the past two years, Pukatawagan has been undergoing massive changes as the conveniences and comforts of the modern world finally make their way to this isolated post.

In the early 1970s, the news media called Pukatawagan the Dodge City of the North. Like other reserve communities across the country, Pukatawagan was suffering from heightened tensions triggered by abject poverty. Houses were nothing more than plywood sheds heated by wood stoves.

There was no electricity, few telephones, no running water. Shooting incidents were common, and drunkenness appeared to be an established way of life. In 1974, band leaders moved to stop the community's downward slide. In an event that has become almost a legend among residents, leaders gathered up all the guns and threw them into the Churchill River, banned liquor from the reserve, and promised to bring changes.

Fourteen years passed before these promises bore fruit. At the end of the 1980s, new homes were being built at a phenomenal rate. There was a new community centre. And more importantly, there was hope within the people that the future would bring many more benefits.

The reserves scattered across Canada are the embodiment of the native drive for self-government. During the past twenty years, changes on reserves have reflected the successes and failures of the ongoing attempts of Indian bands to gain control over their lives. The patterns of change have varied widely across the country. Some reserves, like Pukatawagan, have found themselves taking bold steps forward, only to slip back momentarily before struggling forward again. Others have moved forward with steady strides.

Two hundred kilometres directly south of Pukatawagan is the Cree community of The Pas. It is one of the most prosperous bands in Canada, thanks in part to a 20,000-square-metre shopping mall, and the vision of the band leaders twenty years ago. In 1968, the band employed three people and had a budget of $20,000. The Pas (pronounced "paw") was a shanty town located across the Saskatchewan River from the prosperous non-native community of the same name. Now the band is the area's second largest employer outside of the local pulp and paper operation and has assets worth $21 million and an annual cash flow of $17 million. It employs more than 250 people, native and non-native, and reserve housing looks like any new subdivision in a thriving community. This reserve is typical of about 200 bands across Canada that are situated near urban centres where living conditions are generally better. Their proximity to urban centres allows the bands to take ·

advantage of the non-native economy — better jobs, better access to materials, better housing, for example.

Band Chief Oscar Lathlin says few people could have imagined the changes that have occurred on The Pas reserve during the past twenty years. And no one, he insists, should rule out the potential for similar change and growth in any Indian community. "Twenty years ago our critics could not make any sense of what we wanted to do," Lathlin says. Non-native people predicted that the mall would fail, that it would not be able to compete with the stores across the river, and that whites would refuse to shop there. Although the downtown core of the town of The Pas scratches to survive, the mall, like malls everywhere, is a success, regularly attracting shoppers from across the river and the surrounding area.

## Pattern for Failure

By its own accounting, Ottawa has spent more than $26 billion on Indian reserves during a twenty-year period from 1967-68 to 1987-88. Almost 274,000 people now live on reserves, which is 61 per cent of the total registered Indian population. On average, registered Indians are younger than the Canadian population as a whole. According to data compiled by the Department of Indian Affairs using its own statistics and the 1986 census, 64 per cent of the reserve population is under the age of twenty-five, compared to 40 per cent for the overall Canadian population. And this trend is expected to continue beyond the year 2001. The average income on reserves is about $9,300 less than half of the national average. More than 66 per cent of Indians of working age are either unemployed or on welfare, and that percentage is higher on the isolated reserves. Only 5 per cent have graduated from high school. Odds are high that many will become alcoholics and many will die a violent death. What has that $26 billion brought Indian people?

In 1966, only one in ten reserve houses had central heating. At the end of the 1980s, three out of ten homes still had no furnace. Twenty years ago, 12 per cent of the homes had indoor toilets. That figure is now up to 66 per cent. The percentage of homes with running water has risen from 14 to 75 per cent.

However, more than a quarter of the houses need major repairs, even though the bulk of them were built within the past twenty years.

Ottawa began a big push to improve reserve housing in 1977 when Canada Mortgage and Housing Corporation (CMHC) became a partner with Indian Affairs to provide programs and low-cost loans to spur construction. In 1987, CMHC conducted a survey to access the impact of that involvement. The report, *CMHC On-Reserve Housing Programs*, concluded that, although the financial commitment had been substantial — $1 billion between 1977 and 1987 — the results were mixed. Houses were still crowded, in bad physical condition, and lacked basic amenities. The CMHC report, based on a survey of ninety-four reserves, found that 36 per cent of on-reserve homes were crowded, as opposed to 2.3 per cent of all homes in Canada (CMHC defined "crowding" as a home where parents share a bedroom with their children and where boys and girls over the age of five share the same bedroom), 43 per cent of on-reserve homes were in need of major repair, compared to 13 per cent of houses throughout Canada. CMHC loans to improve housing conditions — in the $5,000 to $8,250 range — were inadequate, the report stated, and would have to be doubled to be effective. The report projected that, if spending continued at the same rate, on-reserve housing conditions would not reach acceptable levels until the year 2010.

Half of Canada's reserve Indians are members of 484 bands with populations of less than 1,000 residents. Eighty-six bands, ranging in size between 1,000 and 3,000 residents, account for 40 per cent of the total population. Indian Affairs classifies a third of the bands as urban, those located within fifty kilometres of a major centre. The department has inappropriately labelled 100 bands as special access, which is a puzzling term because they remain inaccessible except by air. Another 270 bands are classified as rural, which means they are located between 50 and 350 kilometres from a major centre and have year-round road access. The remaining twenty-five are classified as remote; these are located more than 350 kilometres from the nearest centre but are only accessible during the winter months

when paths are cleared over frozen lakes and bogs (this number
slowly dwindles as road construction occurs).

Registered Indians on a reserve are entitled to housing,
education, and health care paid for by the federal government.
Band members are assigned a number at birth by Indian Affairs
so Ottawa can keep track of them. So long as they stay on the
reserve, band members do not pay taxes of any sort. But they
do not own anything either — not the house they live in nor
the land it is built on. The reserve does not belong to Indians;
it is federal land set aside for their use. This makes it impossible
for band members to take out a loan because they have nothing
to offer as collateral.

The first reserves appeared about 160 years ago. As the
British and later the Canadian governments colonized the West,
it became apparent that Indians were getting in the way. In
1830 these mostly nomadic tribes were placed on reserves. The
various Indian forms of government were outlawed, and in
1884 the new Canadian government forced native bands to
elect their leaders.

All bands are now governed by an elected chief and council.
Their job is to administer the funds Ottawa provides for education, housing, and welfare. Until recently, Ottawa alone determined how much money each band was given and in which
areas it would be spent. Throughout most of the 1970s, when
Indian leaders were only beginning to articulate their vision of
a new future, band councils functioned as mere government
administrators, accountable more to Ottawa than to the people
who elected them. There was never enough money for housing,
education, and economic development. Band members would
complain and demand more services; the councils would over-
spend and go into debt in a pattern that was repeated over and
over again across Canada. Ottawa would chastise them and
withhold funds from the next budget to cover the debt. It was
a downward spiral with the poverty feeding on itself.

In the late 1980s, in response to growing and more effective
pressures for greater Indian autonomy, Ottawa loosened its grip
on reserve communities. A handful of bands that Indian Affairs
rated as sophisticated and financially responsible were allowed

to administer global budgets. They were given a lump sum over a five-year period and permission to determine how the money would be spent. But, again, the total budget was set by a formula chosen by Ottawa. Except for a few bands — such as The Pas and some in Alberta that earn royalties from oil and the urban bands whose landholdings around Vancouver have made them wealthy — Ottawa remains the only source of revenue.

In 1984, Indians realized that, despite the gains they had made over the past few decades, Ottawa had still not come on side and was as willing to apply the brakes to their efforts as they had numerous times before. The cause of their fears was the federally initiated Nielsen Task Force report. It concluded that spending by Indian Affairs to support communities in isolated areas, which would never have survived under normal conditions, did nothing more than drain Indians of all initiative and Ottawa of desperately needed funds. "The net impact of government stewardship over the social and economic development of native people has been frustratingly marginal. Program innovations have produced isolated improvements, but the overall picture remains bleak." The report's solution was to stop spending, cap funds, and force the bands to find money for anything above newly established minimum standards or let the community collapse. It recommended that new programs encourage young people to move to prosperous reserves where there were more economic opportunities. With these proposals, the report's authors revealed again that Ottawa did not understand what the Indian leaders wanted.

"The economists believe that you got to go where the market is, that you follow where the jobs are and you never stay in an isolated or rural area because there are no jobs there," says Konrad Sioui, chief of the Secretariat of First Nations of Quebec. "On an economic point of view, that might be true, but realistically it has nothing to do with the Indian vision of their territory, their land, and their role, that Indian people have to play with the land."

The reserve, which started as a tool of a colonizing power, now is a symbol of Indian independence and epitomizes all native self-government aspirations. Bands are now called First Nations, and Indian leaders want to control everything that happens within their boundaries. When Ottawa began transferring program delivery to bands twenty years ago, band officials took advantage of the situation and mastered budgets and local administration. They learned to play the rules according to Ottawa. Now they want their own rules.

"Indian people have survived for 400 years because we haven't given in," says Louis Stevenson, the charismatic leader of the Manitoba Indians. "We've held on to those beliefs — that we have the right to be ourselves, a right to run our own lives, determine our own future. That is what is going to ensure our society survives."

Stevenson is chief of the Peguis reserve, just north of Winnipeg. He is articulate and an expert at media manipulation. During the past ten years, he has established himself as a national leader, heading demonstrations dressed in traditional Indian head-dress and moccasins and several times occupying the Winnipeg offices of Indian Affairs. He gained international recognition in 1987 when he invited the South African ambassador to Canada, Glenn Babb, to visit the Peguis reserve. His goal was to clearly link the way Canada has treated its aboriginal people with the apartheid system of South Africa. If the level of media attention surrounding the event was any indication, the ploy worked.

Indian leaders now want to assume the same powers other governments enjoy. Many are calling for the right to levy taxes on their people, to take on responsibility for new initiatives in lotteries and gambling, wildlife management, policing and justice, child welfare and education. They argue that there is no need any longer for a mammoth bureaucracy to look after their needs because they are capable of doing it themselves. "When we're talking about establishing self-government, we're not talking about diminishing standards but simply taking over control of standards and rebuilding standards that are culturally appropriate to us," says Joe Miskokomon, Grand Chief of the Union of Ontario Indians. "What we're talking about is the utilization of existing resources in a better way."

During the summer of 1988, Pukatawagan was offering hope and change to its residents. The band council had recently opened a $2 million community centre which housed its administrative offices, a post office, laundromat, grocery and general store, small restaurant and eight-room hotel. They had built twenty new homes the previous winter, another twenty were nearing completion, there were plans to build thirty more homes the following year. The houses, built by a southern Manitoba construction firm, are far superior to the shacks which were built in the past. The five-bedroom homes are valued at $80,000 each. They are all connected to running water, sewer lines, hydro, and telephone. They are equipped with four appliances, carpeting, a finished basement, and one and a half baths. There are currently plans to build a bakery, a gas station, and a tourist lodge to take advantage of the reserve's resort setting.

However, these signs of progress and prosperity are misleading. If residents of the reserve don't work for the band council or the few band-owned enterprises, they don't work at all. More than 70 per cent of the Puk residents collect welfare. In fact, almost all money on the reserve comes from Ottawa. Everything from salaries for band councillors and staff to program funding and construction payments for houses and band facilities is federally funded. Even the salaries and shelter allowances which cover the rent all originate from Ottawa.

According to the 1986 census, the number of Canada's native people who relied on some kind of government assistance to live increased during the 1980s. In 1985, the total number of registered Indians on social assistance stood at 45 per cent, which is two and a half times the Canadian average.

For many reserve residents, the politics of self-government and economic development schemes are not such pressing issues in a world where feeding a family or getting a job is their first concern. Yvonne Caribou doesn't know what the future holds for her family in Pukatawagan. "I don't plan that far ahead." Now twenty-five, she has been married for eight years and has three children between the ages of four and eight. "I would like my children to finish school, go to university. I hope

they come back and will be able to find a job here." Yvonne
has been working at the Hudson's Bay general store for more
than a year. It is her first full-time job.

Oliver Colomb runs the pool hall in Pukatawagan, but he
hopes at least some of his children will make their future
elsewhere. "I hope two of my kids will take over the business
some day, but I don't want them all to live on the reserve when
they're older." Thirty-seven-year-old Oliver has five children
between the ages of three and fourteen. He has operated the
pool hall for five years. Before that he hauled freight for seven
years. Although life on the reserve gets better every year, he
says it is still no place for anyone who doesn't have a job.
"That's what I'd expect of my children, too. There's too much
welfare here and not enough jobs."

## Broken Promises

Data supplied by Census Canada and Indian Affairs show that
between 1966 and 1986, the population growth on reserves
matched that of the general Canadian population — a 27 per
cent increase. However, thousands of people fled the reserves
during this period and moved to the city seeking better opportunities. The population of registered Indians living in urban
centres increased from 44,000 in 1966 to 170,000 in 1988. Up
to 23,000 of them are now expected to return, prompted in part
by the apparent prosperity on reserves and by the guarantees
promised by recent federal legislation. Indians who have either
a high school or a university education now find reserve life
attractive. Often they possess the skills others lack and can
expect to become band administrators, one of the few well-
paying jobs available. They can also escape racist attitudes
which persist outside the reserve boundaries.

In the 1880s, Ottawa policy-makers decided that an Indian
woman who married a non-native should no longer be entitled
to the rights enjoyed by all other registered Indians. That
remained Ottawa's policy for 100 years, until it was challenged
by a determined young Micmac Indian woman from New
Brunswick. Like thousands of other native women, Sandra
Lovelace was denied her right to education, housing, and health

care because of her marriage. Rebuffed by the bureaucrats and the courts, Sandra Lovelace finally took her case to the United Nations. Its Human Rights Committee ruled in 1981 that Canada's policy was discriminatory and was denying Indian women and their children rights they were entitled to as Indian people. Buoyed by the U.N. decision, native women organizations intensified their lobbying efforts. Embarrassed by the international condemnation of its policy, Ottawa amended the Indian Act in 1985 with the passage of Bill C-31, ending the legislation's discriminatory aspects.

Studies by Indian Affairs in 1988 estimated that Bill C-31 would increase the status Indian population by 25 per cent, and that 21 per cent of these people would return to the reserves during a five-year period, adding another 23,000 residents. These figures, which many Indian organizations considered too low, were higher than Ottawa's original estimates. The impact of the miscalculation stretched the demand for existing services on reserves and created a situation for which Ottawa refused to take financial responsibility. When Ottawa first introduced Bill C-31 it promised additional funds would be provided to prevent any band from suffering because of the impact of an increased population on already stretched resources. Despite Ottawa's assurances, Bill C-31 made everything worse.

Ottawa appeared to be caught by surprise by the large number of people who applied to regain their status. According to a secret government discussion paper, which was obtained and released in 1988 by the Canadian Press news agency, senior bureaucrats had given politicians two scenarios of Bill C-31's impact: either a 10 per cent or a 20 per cent increase in the registered Indian population. The Mulroney cabinet accepted the lower figure and allocated funds accordingly. Indian groups claimed that the decision to use the lower number was an attempt by Ottawa to reduce the extra funds that would be needed for housing, education, social assistance, and health care to accommodate the growing Indian population. They were right.

The secret discussion paper obtained by the Canadian Press also predicted that new status applicants living in urban centres would put increased pressure for services on the departments of Indian Affairs and Health and Welfare. Additional pressures would be placed on Canada Employment for new training programs and on Canada Mortgage and Housing for greater mortgage assistance. It also predicted there would be greater demands for post-secondary education funding.

Data analysis provided by Health and Welfare to the *Winnipeg Free Press* in April 1988 confirmed Ottawa's concern for increased costs. The department was projecting that the increase in the status Indian population caused by Bill C-31 would create serious funding shortfalls in its Indian programming budgets, producing a deficit of $1.8 million in 1987-88 climbing to $73.4 million by 1990-91.

In the spring of 1989, a year after Ottawa released its Bill C-31 studies, Indian Affairs placed a cap on post-secondary education, freezing funding at $130 million annually and effectively forcing thousands of Indian students to drop out or postpone their studies. Yet again, Ottawa showed that it would opt out of its commitments to native people whenever it had to back that support with additional funding.

## Another World

Life is expensive on an isolated reserve. Most goods are shipped north by rail, bumping up their price tag considerably, while salaries and welfare payments remain tied to southern equivalents. The Hudson's Bay stores, the first meeting places of Indian fur trappers and white traders, still basically retain their monopoly by being the only general store on many remote reserves. During the summer of 1988, groceries that cost $81 at a Winnipeg Safeway totalled $141 at the Hudson's Bay general store in Pukatawagan. A city dweller on a weekly shopping trip would be shocked to find the 425 mL of infant formula that cost $1.94 in Winnipeg was going for $3.17 in Pukatawagan. A ten-kilogram bag of flour was $13.35, more than twice the price of $5.87 in Winnipeg. A four-kilogram bag of sugar in Pukatawagan was selling for $6.26, while in Winnipeg it was less than half at $2.98. Two litres of 2 per cent milk that cost $1.76 in Winnipeg would cost a mother $3.12 in

Pukatawagan. And regular ground beef was three times more expensive, $6.99 per kilogram in Pukatawagan compared to $1.94 per kilogram in Winnipeg.

When Manitoba Hydro built its power line to Pukatawagan a few years ago, wiring the entire community, it brought with it satellite TV. Almost every house on the reserve, new and old, now has a colour television. Culture from the small box consists of the CBC, a movie channel, and American sports and country music channels. White supervisors who work on the reserve say many of the residents, adults and children alike, stay up until three or four in the morning watching television. Since most residents do not work, life does not get under way until 11 a.m. or later.

The violence that engulfed Canada's reserves in the early 1970s was only one form of the devastation that took hold in Indian communities as a result of Ottawa's attempt to shape Indian people into "acceptable citizens." Welfare programs robbed them of their self-esteem, and the education and child welfare policies carried out by white administrators made them feel ashamed of being Indian. Many turned to drinking to numb their pain and anguish, and the drinking led to violence.

Despite efforts to regain control of their lives, drinking remains a problem in Pukatawagan. However, its victims, the drinkers and their often neglected and abused children, are mostly ignored. The overriding feeling in the community is: if the drunks don't shoot anyone or burn anything down, leave them alone.

From her second-storey office overlooking the main street, Caroline Dumas can see the drunks stumble through town and the children who go hungry and cold because their parents are too drunk to look after them. Fifty-four-year-old Caroline was hired as an alcohol- and drug-abuse counsellor after she had been on the wagon for a year. She got the co-ordinator's job when her boss went on a drinking binge and never came back. Caroline was a heavy drinker for eighteen years. Though she has not touched a drop for the past ten years, six of her thirteen children have serious drinking and drug problems, and she knows it is her fault. "They don't listen to me when I talk to them. The more I try to help them, the more they try to hurt me. They tell me, 'You don't drink now, but you used to be a terrible drinker. You didn't care about us or anyone. You hurt us. So what do you expect us to do?'"

Caroline says she cannot erase the memory of what changed her life. It was January 1973. She was thirty-eight. "My husband and I had been drinking all weekend, for four days. I woke up on a Monday morning, but I didn't know where I was or what day it was. I wanted to go home and check on my children, but my husband wanted to stay because there were five more whiskeys and a case of two-four left. When I got home, I found my two youngest sitting on the floor. It was cold, minus forty degrees outside. There was no fire in the house. The two girls were one and two years old then. The youngest one had a bowl between her legs. She mixed together flour, sugar, and cold water. She was so hungry she was eating it, even though it was almost frozen."

Many bands tried to stem the violence by banning alcohol on their reserves. The banning was easier to accomplish on remote reserves where the nearest liquor outlet was a plane-ride away. It was impossible to enforce on reserves with easy access to urban centres. Regardless of a reserve's location, there was always someone willing to profit by a friend's dependence.

After the famous gun-throwing incident in 1974 and a declaration of prohibition, Pukatawagan reverted back to being a "wet" reserve in 1978. The chief and council had realized their attempts at prohibition only forced people to drink in the bushes, which led to more accidents as they struggled home. Band officials say the drinking problem is not as bad as it used to be. Caroline Dumas is not convinced.

"Wet or dry, it doesn't make any difference. People have nothing to do here. Especially the young people. There is no recreation program, and the school gym is closed all summer. They have no place to go." Caroline says the children start drinking as early as six years of age. They also smoke marijuana and sniff glue, contact cement, nail polish, felt markers, and gasoline. "The kids sleep all day at school because they've been up all night drinking or sniffing."

A non-native group-home worker says bootleggers regularly take the train north to Lynn Lake on a Friday night and return the next day with a full box car. "They come back Saturday morning with hundreds of cases of beer wrapped in green garbage bags. No one says anything but everyone knows what's inside the garbage bags." A twelve-pack of beer sells for $40 and a twenty-four-ounce bottle of liquor costs $60.

Like many reserves across Canada, Pukatawagan assumed control of its local school program in the mid-1980s. An education committee, similar to a school board, hires the teaching and support staff and has been trying to develop a curriculum that will keep the reserve's children in school. Across the country, Indian students have higher drop-out rates than non-natives and score lower in their grade exams. Only 5 per cent graduate from high school, and 40 per cent never make it beyond Grade 8. Almost all the students are at least one year behind in their grade level and begin their first year unable to speak English.

Pukatawagan and other reserves like it need more motivated teachers willing to work closely with the children, with studies that reflect Indian tradition, customs, and history. But the reserve's education committee is hampered by a budget controlled by Ottawa, which means it has no money to hire properly trained staff or develop classroom programs necessary to keep the children in school. However, Pukatawagan has reduced the drop-out rate in the lower grades. Before it took over its education program, half of the students would routinely drop out by the end of the school year. At the end of 1988, local officials had managed to almost eliminate the drop-out problem.

## We Have a Dream

A long way from the Ottawa headquarters of the Assembly of First Nations, where strategists map out the next steps for Indian leaders and their self-government dreams, Alex Bighetty takes life one day at a time. A clerk at the Pukatawagan Bay store, twenty-seven-year-old Alex is married with two small children. "I don't know what will happen here in five or ten years." He would like his children to attend school off the reserve. "They'd get a better education, but I'd want them to come back and apply what they learned to make Pukatawagan a better place." Like many of his friends, Alex expects to spend the rest of his life in Pukatawagan.

Canada has held the Indian's hand for over 100 years. It has broken the native spirit by attempting to force assimilation by using schools and laws to try to eradicate native customs and traditions. But the Indians have never forgotten who they are. Their leaders eventually learned to take advantage of the programs Ottawa offered, to manage multi-million-dollar budgets, to develop and implement reserve programs for housing, road construction, and social assistance. All the band governments have taken on the responsibilities of a typical Canadian municipality, and more. Half of the bands in Canada now run their own school programs and are preparing to take over health care. Unlike municipalities, however, bands are unincorporated and still exist only as creations of the federal government. Some have resorted to "monster bingo" games to supplement federal revenues. On rare occasions, bands like The Pas have convinced Ottawa of the merits of business ventures whose profits can be used to provide needed services in the community. Indian leaders, often with the help of private business, have devised ways to raise money to break their dependency on Ottawa. Now they want Ottawa to release its grip on their people.

"If we listen to all the scepticism from non-natives, I'm afraid that twenty years from now we're going to be in the same boat," Chief Oscar Lathlin says. Life can change for everyone, he insists, and The Pas is proof of that. "Each reserve will evolve on its own. I wish we could go to a northern reserve in twenty years and see how far they've come. We have a vision. We have a dream. If we persist, if we don't give up, twenty years from now it's going to be a lot different, a lot better."

# 3

# Urban Indians

They are called bus refugees. Every year thousands of native Canadians travel by plane, bus, and rickety automobile from their remote or rural reserves into the country's major city centres, carrying with them their personal belongings and hopes for a better life than the poverty-stricken one they have left behind. What they have found more often than not in these concrete jungles is a world where they are unwelcome, where their facial features, accents, hair-styles, history, and way of thinking keep them apart from other city dwellers, a world where they exist in a political vacuum, the responsibility of no one in particular and considered the burden of many.

Statistics Canada has gathered hard cold facts that show that Indians who live off reserves can expect to be a little more educated and make a little more money than those who live on reserves. However, these benefits do not necessarily mean that the good life awaits them in city centres. According to the 1986 census, the average income for the 134,910 registered Indians who lived off reserves was $11,000, compared to $9,300 for those living on reserves. But these figures compare to a non-native average individual income of $18,188, which leaves Indians, no matter where they lived, far behind everyone else. As well, data compiled by Statistics Canada in 1986 show that Indians who lived off reserves had the highest percentage of unemployed among all aboriginal groups, 17 per cent or two and a half times the Canadian rate of 7 per cent. The off-reserve figure is almost twice the 9 per cent average cited in the 1981 census for the same group and higher than the on-reserve unemployment rate of 15 per cent.

Education, cited by both native and non-native people alike as a key to changing Indian fortunes, is another depressing indicator. In the five years between 1981 and 1986, the number of Indians over the age of fifteen with less than a Grade 9 education remained twice the national rate. However, there were some signs of hope on reserves. Indian education initiatives, including band-run schools, seem to be having some impact: the figure of reserve Indians with less than a Grade 9 education declined fractionally. However, off-reserve figures show virtually no improvement. In 1981, 24.3 per cent of off-reserve Indians aged fifteen or over had less than a Grade 9 education compared to 24.4 per cent in 1986. This compares to Canadian figures of 20.1 per cent and 17.3 per cent respectively.

The picture painted by all these numbers is not hard to recognize for anyone who has walked through any of the slums of Regina, Winnipeg, Vancouver, or even the small towns of northwestern Ontario. On the streets is the reality: young native prostitutes hanging around the seedy bars only a few blocks north of Winnipeg's famous Portage and Main intersection; the overactive soup kitchens of Regina's core area feeding primarily native children; the endless stream of drunk and drugged Indians staggering along the streets of northern Ontario towns.

Eastern visitors on inaugural trips through western Canada often comment, with some surprise, at the number of Indian residents, particularly in the city centres. They are also often taken aback by how much of a toll this group is obviously taking on all social service agencies, jails, and unemployment lines.

Although the actual number of registered Indians is the highest in British Columbia and Ontario (54,100 and 46,725 respectively in 1986), a different picture emerges when the ranking is ordered according to the proportion of native Canadians in a particular province or region. For example, Manitoba and Saskatchewan have the highest proportion of

registered Indians (outside of the Yukon and Northwest Territories with rates of 12.7 and 14.3 per cent respectively).
Quebec at 0.4 per cent has the smallest ratio, followed closely
by the Maritime provinces and Ontario at 0.5 per cent. In 1986,
Saskatchewan's 42,075 Indians accounted for 4.2 per cent of
that province's total population. Manitoba's figure stood at 3.8.
(In fact, all figures are actually somewhat higher. In 1986, 136
reserves, accounting for about 45,000 people, did not participate in the census.) Winnipeg and Regina have the largest
urban Indian populations in the country.

A major influx of reserve Indians into major urban centres
was predicted in the late 1960s by Harry Hawthorn in his
two-volume study for the federal government, *A Survey of
Contemporary Indians in Canada.* "Special facilities will be
needed to ease the process of social adjustments as the tempo
of off reserve movement increases," warned Hawthorn. And
for the most part, Hawthorn's predictions have held true. Between 1966 and 1986, the numbers of Canadian off-reserve
Indians jumped 254 per cent — from 47,496 to 158,944 —
while the reserve population grew by only 27 per cent. According to the 1986 census, 38 per cent of Canada's registered
Indian population lived off reserves. Projections to the year
2001 put the off-reserve population at 237,400.

Observers of federal policy began issuing warnings to Ottawa about the impact of Bill C-31 on Indians as soon as the
policy was announced in the mid-1980s. Bill C-31 followed a
1981 decision by the United Nations Human Rights Committee
which condemned the discriminatory practice of removing
status rights from any Indian woman who married a non-Indian. A report based on the 1986 census indicates that 91,000
Bill C-31 Indians could be expected to join the registered
Indian ranks, most of them city dwellers. The census analysis
predicted that the impact of Bill C-31 on the overall urban
Indian population would peak between 1985 and 1990, with
the population figures jumping 17.3 per cent in 1986. By 1996,
this impact should all but disappear. The analysts, who have
been criticized by Indian leaders for underestimating the Bill

C-31 impact, predicted that off-reserve population growth would fall to 1.2 per cent by 1996.

## Choosing to Stay

What this means for Indians is that those who moved to the cities after losing their status will have the option of returning home and taking advantage of the housing, education, and tax benefits extended to all registered Indians. Those who choose to stay in cities, and these are predicted to be the majority, will continue to turn to the federal, provincial, and municipal governments for services. The impact of all this on western Canada, where about 80 per cent of the country's Indian population is concentrated, has been especially profound in the urban setting. In Manitoba, for example, the urban Indian population jumped 330 per cent (by conservative estimates) between 1966 and 1986. In Winnipeg, the downtown core is considered home to an estimated 60,000 native people, and according to predictions, that number will hit 100,000 by the next century. It is a story repeated across the Canadian West.

The migration to cities, however, has not been a steady tidal wave and has been less than what Hawthorn and others predicted it would be in the late 1960s. Improvements to reserve housing, a recognition that city life was no picnic, and employment opportunities from successful economic development projects on reserves had slowed the wave somewhat by the end of the 1980s.

These factors and others have led to the birth of something city planners refer to as a "hypermobile" population. With houses and some job hopes on the reserves and few opportunities in the urban setting, Indians have slowly come to establish two home bases. Home is in the city during winter months where welfare benefits, including heated accommodations and running water, make life at least physically manageable. And then it's back to the reserve to see family and friends and to live the more traditional life during the summer when hunting and fishing can offset meagre welfare payments and the high costs of living.

This "hypermobility" is just one of the reasons why determining how many Indians, status or otherwise, are living within the country's major urban settings has proven so difficult. In Winnipeg, a city with one of the largest downtown Indian populations in North America, the numbers of registered Indians can vary between 18,000, a figure quoted by various government sources, and 30,000, the estimate of urban Indian organizations. The number jumps to 60,000 when all aboriginal people, regardless of official status, are included.

The fact that no one can say with any degree of accuracy just how many Indians live in Canadian cities highlights what is probably the key urban Indian issue for the 1990s — whose responsibility are they? At the time of Confederation, there was considerable debate over who would oversee the needs of all Indians and Indian land, the provincial governments or Ottawa. The federal government ended up playing such a large role partly because most Indians at the time lived in federal territory and few provincial agencies had enough expertise to respond to the complex needs of the population.

However, the issue of who should be responsible for Indians who moved into urban settings had been debated for decades and remained officially unresolved in the late 1980s. "There are responsibilities from the provincial side for supplying the same services to Indian people as they do non-Indians," insisted former Indian Affairs Minister Bill McKnight in 1988, echoing a statement made twenty years earlier by then Indian Affairs Minister Jean Chrétien. Not so, said newly elected Manitoba Premier Gary Filmon. Filmon was echoing the opinion of most provincial leaders across the country. "I would argue that the federal government still has responsibility for [urban Indians]," Filmon said, adding that providing education, training, and child welfare services for such a needy group would be an expensive proposition. "It will create a massive drain on the provincial treasury."

And the debate doesn't end there with politicians and bureaucrats. Indian leaders across the country are also pondering the questions of jurisdiction. On one side of their debate are those who contend that Indians should maintain control over the administration of services to their people, no matter where they live. "Urban Indians should continue to come under the jurisdiction of their bands," says Saul Terry, head of the Union of British Columbia Indians. Terry argues that having the provinces take over services for urban Indians fits too closely to the long-held federal plan to get the provincial governments more involved, a scheme that must be resisted as part of the overall drive for native self-government.

In Terry's mind, band authority should simply extend from reserve to city, with Indian housing and child welfare authorities doing the same work for the urban dwellers as they do for their reserve constituents. "Most of the provinces do not know or understand the responsibilities of the federal government," says Chief Roland Crowe of the Saskatchewan Federation of Indians as a warning to those provincial leaders who have expressed some willingness to consider stepping in. "The premiers feel good sitting around the table with the big boys, but they'd better think twice about what responsibility for Indian people means."

On the other side of the native debate are Indian leaders who see the eventual emergence of urban Indian associations that closely mimic band and reserve structures, but that exist as separate legislated authorities. "Because we are receiving provincial funding for urban people, we have to come to an agreement with the province, the feds, and also with urban government," says Lyle Longclaws of Winnipeg's U.oan Indian Association. "That is key, and different from what the chiefs are pursuing rurally." In Longclaws's vision of the urban Indian world, band councils would be responsible for residents who moved away, but after a period of time, these city dwellers would fall under the jurisdiction of new urban Indian groups. These urban Indian associations would lobby for special legislation that would allow them to govern urban Indian populations. In this scenario, urban Indian child welfare agencies would be established, as would urban Indian educational authorities.

Some movement in this direction has already begun. Early in 1990, Winnipeg native leaders began seriously lobbying for their own school board and school. They got a very cool reception but gave no sign of giving up.

When Indians first started to leave their reserves, probably not long after signing treaties with the British government in the late nineteenth century, their numbers were small. "Either you had to move to a reserve to receive your rations because the buffalo were gone and there was no food source, or you were forced to urbanize or become civilized by moving closer together," says one urban Indian. Initially, Indians who trekked to the cities were almost entirely absorbed; those who could not assimilate returned home, or got dragged down into the underbelly of the urban ghettos.

However, as their numbers began to grow, municipal and provincial government programs began popping up as a matter of necessity. Social service agencies handled the first trickle of cases that came to their attention. Eventually, native friendship centres opened and acted as focal points for the growing number of Indians finding their way into the cities. The numbers began increasing at an accelerated rate during the 1960s, and the issue of who was ultimately responsible for providing services to this group became a more pressing issue. The piecemeal approach of the past was no longer enough, and the chorus of demands couldn't be ignored.

## Growing Tensions
In the midst of these growing tensions emerged a number of urban native associations, some representing all aboriginal people within their city's boundaries, and others lobbying only for the more narrowly defined status or registered Indians. Throughout the 1980s, the building up and tearing down of urban Indian associations continued with a vengeance, and will likely continue. Although native people across the country have emerged during the past few decades with a clearer sense of their common goal of self-government, urban natives have not. When the national leadership calls for a demonstration, thousands of Indians across the country respond, but a similar call by an urban association in Winnipeg in 1989 drew barely thirty people. Is this kind of poor showing the result of the

associations' contradictory mandates and troubled sense of direction? Or is it the result of extreme poverty? Urban Indians are among the poorest of the poor, and may simply be too busy surviving to worry about the intricacies and demands of effective lobbying.

"Natives come in and they are not aware of politics," says Stan Fulham, former secretary for the Manitoba Métis Federation and head of a native housing co-operative. He is talking about the hundreds of native people each year who land on his doorstep seeking aid. "They are disorganized. They require organizations, like the Urban Indian Association, to crystallize their problems and to convey on a continuing basis the story of their economic and social isolation to government."

The 1969 White Paper proposed the abolition of special status for Indians, suggesting that assimilation into the greater Canadian context was the answer to native poverty and discrimination. But in the city centres, where this assimilation theory has been put to the real test, it has become clear that there are no simple answers. Though some native people move to the city, find a job, and live happily ever after, they are lost among the thousands who do not.

From impoverished conditions on reserves, Canada's native citizens move into the city centres only to find themselves at the bottom of an even larger heap. "I don't know how they get here," said a Manitoba native housing worker. "They just end up here." With few work skills, particularly in an increasingly technical society, language barriers, different work habits and ways of looking at the world, they usually end up on skid row. One young native woman told a CBC radio show host that, despite the deplorable and unsafe conditions in the downtown core, it was still home to her. "Once you're down here ... it is where all your friends are." She went on to describe the kind of racism that is familiar to all native people.

Stories of racism turned up in dozens of interviews conducted for a special report on Indian issues for the *Winnipeg Free Press* — everything from outright abuse at the hands of police to small daily confrontations with racist attitudes. One native leader, whose husband is a civil servant with a salary that allows them to live a middle-class life, described several examples of the difficulties she found when shopping or being served in restaurants. In one case, she was approached by a sales clerk while examining a pair of $60 running shoes in a sports store and asked if she was aware of just how much those shoes cost. Others shared tales of being followed the minute they entered certain department stores and of being turned down for apartments because they were native people.

Many native people avoid racist confrontations by living together in the ghettoized pockets that every city mysteriously sets aside for them. For many Indian leaders, this ghettoization creates a pattern repeated by many native people when they enter city life. It is a cycle that begins by following friends and family into the bar and drug scene, and turns into a way of life with no escape.

The authors of the 1969 White Paper assumed that, if the Indian Act and the Indian Affairs department were eliminated, equality for Indian people would follow. There was also an assumption that within thirty years Indians throughout the country would be assimilated into the Canadian mainstream as thriving, tax-paying residents of major urban centres. But during the last twenty years, perhaps because of the legislative limbo they have been forced to live in — no specific bureaucracy to co-ordinate services, no leaders to lobby on their behalf, and no legislation to govern them — urban Indians have not benefitted at all. "When you look at the reality, we are far from assimilated," says Longclaws. "We are very much isolated from the rest of Winnipeg society. You know where Indians live in this city, and you don't go beyond those boundaries when you are native."

Native leaders point to Canada's treatment of political refugees to highlight how effective the federal government can be when truly motivated. The situation underlines the discrepancies between what refugees can expect and how the Canadian government and the Canadian people treat native people as they migrate in increasing numbers to the country's urban centres.

Canada has a well-earned international reputation for its outstanding treatment of the thousands of political refugees who arrive here every year. These federally sponsored orphans land on Canadian soil and walk directly into a year-long, all-expenses-paid adjustment program co-ordinated by the federal Department of Employment and Immigration. When the newcomer steps off the airplane, a team of federal employees are waiting, including an interpreter, to help with luggage, customs, and security clearances. The nervous visitor, interpreter in tow, is then whisked off to one of several settlement houses which will be home for the next several weeks.

Clothing needs are assessed immediately and within a few days are filled at tax-payers' expense. All the necessary paperwork for social insurance numbers, health care, etc., is completed. Orientation sessions begin on everything — how to take a bus, how to use money, and where to shop. When an apartment or house is located, furniture needs are assessed and an order is filled. Detailed guidance on how to survive on government subsidies is offered. Usually by this point, the newcomer's sixth month, daily English courses at one of the local colleges have begun. When English courses are completed, the refugee is now deemed to be job ready. Immigration staff stay in touch, however, offering counselling on everything from marital problems to how to access health and other services. Then job hunting and training begin. According to one department official, 90 per cent of refugees spend an average of one year under the wing of the federal government before they find jobs. The 10 per cent who are still searching for work a year after their arrival are then turned over to the city's social services department. Finally, multicultural initiatives, heavily sponsored by all three levels of government, mean that new Canadians likely find some outlet to express their cultural identity — both their emerging one and the one they left behind.

Across Canada, Indians often arrive in cities from remote regions as confused as any refugee. But, instead of one place to start, they are faced with dozens of provincial government departments which might have native programs, a range of municipally sponsored initiatives aimed at the inner-city poor, a growing number of urban Indian associations and housing authorities, and native friendship centres. They will discover that they do not qualify for English-language courses and that even inner-city schools with majority native populations offer little help. If they need to use a bus, a friend or family member has to show them.

## New Programs

As one observer noted, Indians are barely at the starting gate. But some things are changing. During the past twenty years, urban native programs have gone through an interesting and familiar transition. Early attempts to solve the urban aboriginal problem were plagued by a white-dominated bureaucracy that concentrated on short-term solutions to long-term problems. For example, job training programs aimed at native people tended to offer training for short-term employment or to under-train, thus condemning them to begin working at jobs on the lowest rung of the economic ladder. The problem was that, despite training, jobs were impossible to find or were never held for long. Thus the training circuit, complete with a liveable allowance, has become for many native people a job in itself. Once one program is over, another is started. The 1986 census indicates that dependence on government programs (federal, provincial, and municipal), including welfare, unemployment insurance, and family allowance, increased for all aboriginal groups between 1981 and 1986. This included a 16 percentage point increase in the number of off-reserve residents relying on programs, from 25 per cent to 41 per cent.

But many say the evolution of off-reserve services has now reached a second stage, characterized by such joint efforts as the CORE Area initiative in Winnipeg and similar long-term federal, provincial, and municipal plans to revitalize downtown core areas. Because these areas are often heavily populated by native people, much of the programming has involved them. After a slow start, in which training failed to solve the problems, a new approach has emerged, one that has measurably improved the success rates. For example, in one Winnipeg program, native trainees aim at a very specific job that will be available when they graduate.

Another important development, although still in its early stages, has been the on-the-job, informal education of the city's civil servants to help them understand who native Canadians are and what it is they want. Sharon Gould, affirmative action director of the city of Winnipeg, says part of her job is teaching white civil servants about native people. This includes making them aware of the reality beyond the clichés which may form much of their opinion. Her aim is to help these civil servants understand the needs and goals of a wide range of native people, from the undereducated, who are struggling to upgrade their formal education in order to break into the civil service ranks, to the growing native middle class. Gould's program extends to senior management who may be asked to be more flexible with the kind of resources they provide. Help in finding day care may mean the difference between a native woman's success in getting and keeping a city hall clerk job, Gould says. The same applies to helping native trainees deal with difficult spouses who discourage their ambitions or with friends who accuse trainees of selling out because they have taken a job in the white world.

"Native people deal with things holistically," Gould explains when asked about the kinds of things she is learning and passing on in the process. "The education we are trying to do [involves teaching civil servants] that there are native people who are professionals and are quite happy on their own. There are native people who need training and support for awhile, and then they are fine. And then there are people who for a whole bunch of reasons don't really want to be here, but they want to come to work for three or four months and then they want to go back to the reserve. And that's fine too." At the same time, part of the education of the other staff includes the message that not everyone in the country is bent on moving up the corporate ladder and that there is room for them too.

According to Sharon Bertchilde of the CORE Area development project, no one should assume Winnipeg has solved its native problem. And there is plenty of evidence to support that.

After twenty years of dealing with native issues, city recruitment programs have failed to attract any more than a handful of native police officers. In 1988, the 1,140-member force had one officer on the force who listed his nationality as Canadian Indian and a few Métis. Calgary police reported two treaty Indians on their 1,000-member force; Regina boasted seven treaty and Métis officers. The native population of Regina is estimated at about 40,000; Calgary is about a third of that.

"I think we have made a whole bunch of little dents but not anything substantial enough to change the way the world is working," Bertchilde says. "Without some sustained effort, what we have done may disappear." She also points out that, even in the short life of the CORE program, the once strict order of responsibility has shifted. "Suddenly the jurisdictional boundaries that have typically been in place are a little fuzzy." But with fewer arguments over which level of government or which department is responsible for what, there is more room for new solutions.

Perhaps this explains why Manitoba Native Affairs Minister James Downey announced that his government would launch a two-year program aimed at developing a co-ordinated strategy for assisting the province's urban Indians. Manitoba is the first province in the country to take such a bold step, something other jurisdictions have avoided for fear that such interest would signal to Ottawa a willingness to accept financial responsibility. Although the question of who is ultimately responsible still remains unresolved, Downey says that he is not willing to ignore the plight of urban natives while waiting for solutions. "I think, for too long, the native people have been bounced back and forth between jurisdictions and their lives have not been going on." Whether or not this bold step will be followed through, or whether the announcement was simply more of the political posturing that is all too familiar to native Canadians, is another question.

If Downey's plan comes about, urban Indian leaders will heartily welcome the initiative. Certainly it would gather data that would help the urban native associations gain a better grasp of their clientele and how many need services. It might also help them raise their own profiles so that the crystallization of common purpose, an essential ingredient in gaining any power, would begin. The plan would also give Indian leaders a focus within a political vacuum in order to sell the solutions they believe will work.

Like national native groups, urban Indian associations say their primary focus must be education, followed by major economic development strategies leading to jobs for their people. "The various government departments have to start getting a good return for their money," says Calvin Pompana, head of the Urban Indian Association in Winnipeg.

Lyle Longclaws is convinced that reserves will eventually disappear as almost all native people become city dwellers, and that the growing urban native middle class will eventually emerge as the dominant one. Others passionately dispute this, saying that the growing power of Canada's native people will ensure that their lives and their power always stem from the land. But reserves or no reserves, the number of natives in Canada's urban centres will grow. "More and more come into the city every day as bus refugees," says Longclaws. "And they're not going to stop coming."

# 4

# Self-Government

Most Canadians know nothing about the long history of Indian self-government. Before the arrival of the Europeans in the seventeenth century and for a couple of hundred years afterwards, Indian nations, with their own complex institutions of government, existed right across North America — among the west coast Haida and the Salish of interior British Columbia, the nomadic Blood, Blackfoot, and Plains Cree across the prairies, the Hurons and the Six Nations of the Iroquois Confederacy, the Ojibway and Naskapi and James Bay Cree of Central Canada, and the Malecite and Micmacs of the Maritimes.

A common theme runs through various Indian mythologies: laws and customs were given to the Indian people by a supernatural being, and no one can take those away. In the days before European domination, Indian people chose their own leaders according to tradition and followed rules that defined and legitimized their institutions. On the west coast, tribes governed themselves through the potlatch, a gathering of people who, during ceremonies involving song, dances, and speeches, would select their leaders and make decisions. On the other side of the continent, the Iroquois, also known as the Haudenosaunee Confederacy, governed through the longhouse. There was a formalized constitution and a code of laws (that some bands still follow today) which governed the conduct of its people and officials. Male and female leaders were chosen from each family clan and decisions reached through consensus. The confederacy was the model American colonies used for their first union.

Self-government has always been a simple and straightforward concept for aboriginal people. It is their right to govern themselves as they decide, sharing power with Ottawa and the provinces. In the aboriginal view, Indian First Nations should become an integral part of the Canadian federal system, sharing revenues as equals with the provinces and Ottawa, and designing their own social, administrative, and economic institutions.

"A lot of people think Indian people are pursuing the goal of independence, and that's not the case," says Louis Stevenson, chief of the Peguis band in Manitoba and one of the aboriginal movement's national leaders. "I recognize that we live within the country called Canada and its boundaries. So we recognize that Canada is going to be in control over certain matters. We recognize that the province is going to be in control over certain matters. And we recognize that we are in control over certain matters on our own reserves. And where there's overlapping, there's going to be joint sharing of that responsibility with the Canadian or provincial governments."

The Indian vision would alter forever the map of Canada. The twenty-first century would see a country parcelled not only by the provinces and territories but by as many as 596 smaller First Nations (today's Indian bands). The result? A buyer of a new car from an auto dealer on a First Nation's territory would pay sales tax to that band, not to the provincial government. Policemen issuing speeding tickets would wear band or tribal council uniforms; revenue from the tickets would go to a First Nation's justice system or motorists would fight the ticket in a First Nation's court before Indian magistrates. Under the new order, history lessons would teach Indian children the role Harold Cardinal played in the struggle for aboriginal self-government.

More than $26 billion has been spent on Indians during the past twenty years, yet there has been only marginal improvement in overall living conditions for Canada's aboriginal people. Ottawa needs more money and a new political agenda to deal with Indian issues. Indian leaders recognize Ottawa's problem as lack of political will and financial resources; thus taking control of their own programs and revenue sources, they argue, is the only way to change conditions.

Twenty years ago, Ottawa embarked on a devolution policy in response to native demands for self-government. Under this policy, Indian Affairs gradually allowed Indian bands to administer their own programs, beginning with education, housing, and social assistance and later child welfare and policing. But the local band officials who were given the responsibility of looking after their own people were not given any administrative training by Ottawa. As a result, they frequently had problems fulfilling their new duties. To compound the situation, program content and budgets were still dictated by Ottawa. Devolution thus created a cadre of untrained band officials who found themselves unable to do any more than carry out government orders on the reserve. Budget deficits and service delays became routine.

However, band administrators learned from their mistakes. Now it is hard to find any who do not run efficient, municipal-style administrations. University graduates, some who honed their skills working first for Indian Affairs, now hold key band positions. Yet in almost all crucial areas — education, child welfare, justice, health, economic development — Ottawa or the provinces still determine how the programs will be delivered to Indian people and how much money is available for those programs.

## Rulers of Their Own House

For Indian leaders, the next step after devolution is self-government, with Indian governments setting their own priorities and spending accordingly. "When we talk about self-government, we mean the capacity to control our own affairs," says Konrad Sioui, Chief of the Secretariat of First Nations of Quebec. "We don't only mean how we can transfer some authority from the federal or provincial governments."

The dispute surrounding self-government centres on the issue of jurisdiction — specifically, the authority to create laws and establish institutions to carry them out. Until now, Ottawa and the provinces have claimed that they had jurisdiction; all powers exercised by Indian bands have been handed down by Ottawa and approved by provincial governments. In areas like native policing, education, and child welfare, Ottawa agreed to the transfer so long as the Indian organizations agreed to subjugate themselves to provincial authorities. But Indians claim they do not need anyone's permission to run their own lives. With the exception of the past 200 years, they have lived independently for thousands of years. During that 200-year period, first Britain and then Ottawa manipulated the Indian lifestyle and produced only disastrous results. "They took control of our lives, and with the conditions that are prevalent here today, it's quite obvious they failed miserably," says Louis Stevenson. "There was an outright attempt to wipe us off the face of this country, and they failed at that too."

The Indian claim to independence is rooted in the annals of Canadian history. The English and the French formed alliances with Indian nations, first for trade and then as they fought for control of North America. Following the defeat and withdrawal of the French, King George III issued the Royal Proclamation of 1763 which prevented any land settlement until treaties had been negotiated between the Crown and the Indian nations. The revolt of the American colonies forced the English to continue their military alliances with Indian nations until the two countries ended their disputes with the conclusion of the War of 1812. After that the whites no longer needed the Indians — they were just getting in the way.

Treaties were signed with the prairie Indian people as a means of allowing peaceful settlement and development. By 1830, the British introduced the reserve system as part of the treaties. The once nomadic prairie people were gathered up and settled on reserves. The tribes of the west coast and central Canada were also confined to small tracts of land. Their institutions of government, the longhouse and the potlatch, were banned, and all Indians were placed under the wardship of

Indian agents. In 1876, the Canadian Parliament passed the first Indian Act, which strengthened the government's control over Indians and the reserve lands, and imposed for the first time on Indians the concept of an elected band chief and council. Once a people free to roam across the continent, Indians found themselves confined to land that they were allowed to use but could not own.

Since 1980, enshrining aboriginal self-government in the Constitution has been the goal of Indian leaders. Only then will they know that Canada has recognized that aboriginal people have the right to govern themselves without the involvement of Ottawa or the provinces. The concept, raised repeatedly in negotiations, has left both levels of senior government cautious.

During negotiations, Ottawa and the provinces have introduced several stalling tactics, including a demand for a definition of self-government and a specific timetable for the transfer of powers. Indian leaders refuse to give either. Indian traditions vary across the country, and many bands would demand the right to adapt their traditional customs as they see fit within the framework of self-government. Some bands could assume control of their lives now; others lag decades behind in development. Indian leaders want each individual band to determine the timing of its own independence and how broad its powers of jurisdiction will be. Yet, if the right to self-government is accepted, then it could not be denied to any band, regardless of when Ottawa or any other power judged it ready.

Federal support of native programs has always fallen victim to political whims and the economic climate of the day. However, Indian leaders have no illusions about a magic, bottomless source of revenue once they are on their own. Controlling the land and its resources are key to the Indian vision of self-government.

The treaties signed between 1763 and the turn of the twentieth century had different meanings for the Indians and the British and Canadian authorities. The governments saw the treaties as a means of relocating the native population so the land could be cleared for white settlement and development.

But the Indians saw the treaty as a formal agreement between
sovereign states to share the land in return for certain guarantees. Today Indians interpret continued government funding as
partial payment for surrendering their land. Regaining control
of the land is essential to an Indian band's financial future;
having authority to determine what occurs on the land com-
pletes the self-government concept.

But the land also defines what a band is. Indian culture and
tradition is inseparable from the land. Self-government can
only work if the land question is settled at the same time. "We
have our own land base which makes us different from any
so-called cultural group in Canada," says Louis Stevenson.
"That's part of our nationhood as Indian people. We have a full
right to be in control of that territory and all the rights that we
have as an Indian nation."

Indian bands that signed treaties with Ottawa, representing
half of the 444,000 registered Indian population, claim owner-
ship to large tracts of land which Ottawa has yet to give them.
Almost every western band has an outstanding land claim. The
1984 Nielsen Task Force report — a comprehensive review of
all spending on federal programs — estimated the total value
of land claims at $8 billion. The task force recommended that
Ottawa reach an accommodation with the Indian community
on self-government before beginning negotiations to settle the
claims. Indian leaders insist that both issues must be settled
simultaneously and suggest that the solution will have to be
innovative and flexible.

One Indian proposal involves a combination of settling land
claims and assigning federal and provincial contracts exclusively to Indian firms. First Nation communities would be
established near large urban centres, creating industrial com-
plexes to take advantage of existing federal and provincial
projects. Land taxes would be paid to the First Nation government, jobs would be created and people trained, expanding the
tax base of Indian government.

Bands in isolated areas would have to depend on natural
resources — mining, timber, hydro — to finance their
programs. For that to become a reality, they would have to

control development. Under this plan, mining and timber companies would need First Nations approval for their projects. Royalties, which normally go to Ottawa and the provinces, would go directly to the Indian government. "We don't expect anything different than what the rest of society has right now: control over their own lives to control their own future," Stevenson says. "That's what we want."

Some bands would never be able to exploit industrial or resource opportunities because of their location. Their future lies with continued federal support. However, unlike Ottawa's present practice of dictating budgets to bands, several aboriginal models of self-government call for continued federal support in the same way that Ottawa deals with the provinces, through equalization payments. This would alter Ottawa's relationship with Indian bands from ministerial to intergovernmental, removing completely any control or input the federal government has on how Indian funds would be spent.

## Ottawa's Answer

The Nielsen Task Force's recommendation for resolving the self-government question fell far short of what aboriginal people have envisioned for their future. The task force saw no room for a constitutional accommodation of aboriginal people. Instead, its report stated that self-government should remain merely an administrative task with Indian functionaries carrying out duties that Ottawa agrees to transfer to them under provincial supervision. Although Ottawa did not officially endorse the task force findings, subsequent legislation has led Indian leaders to conclude that they are in fact being carried out. It is from this perception that Indian leaders view Ottawa's most publicized self-government trophies, the 1984 James Bay agreement and the 1986 Sechelt agreement. These are held out by Ottawa as potential models for the Indian future. Indian leaders see them only as examples of continued subservience.

In 1984, Ottawa enacted what it claimed to be the first Indian self-government legislation, Bill C-46, the Cree-Naskapi (of Quebec) Act. The legislation represented the culmination of a series of negotiations started nine years earlier involving land claims and cash settlements which allowed for the construction of the mammoth James Bay hydro project in northern Quebec. Under the legislation, land and cash and a degree of self-government were given to eight Cree bands and a Naskapi band. The bands were removed from the control of the Indian Act, and a wide range of powers was transferred to their control.

The bands were incorporated and band councils, with an elected chief and councillors, were legally created. The councils were given the right to make laws affecting land and natural resources, use of buildings, band funds, community development and charitable projects, and the cultural and traditional values of the Cree and Naskapi. The 1984 legislation prevails over all other acts of Parliament, and provincial laws do not apply when they conflict with the Cree-Naskapi Act.

Two years later, Ottawa unveiled its second piece of legislation, the Sechelt Indian Band Self-Government Act. Much of the same powers given to the James Bay communities were also given to the Sechelt band, located on the British Columbia coast, just west of Vancouver. In addition, the Sechelt were given the right to create a constitution establishing the authority of the band council and its powers. However, the constitution had to be approved by Ottawa before it could come into force. Several months after Ottawa passed the Sechelt Act, the B.C. government also passed its own Sechelt legislation. It recognized the band council as the governing body of the area, thus allowing the band to exercise all powers that the province grants to it.

Unlike with the James Bay communities, there was no land claims settlement with the Sechelt. Although the legislation takes precedence over most federal laws, the Sechelt band is still subject to two key pieces of federal legislation governing natural resources: the Indian Oil and Gas Act and the British Columbia Indian Reserves Mineral Resources Act. In addition, the band does not have the authority to control lotteries and gambling within its borders.

From a non-native perspective, both pieces of legislation appear to fulfil the aboriginal goal of self-government. It would appear that Ottawa and the provinces of Quebec and British Columbia have created working examples of municipal-style governments, with broader powers affecting culture and natural resources. And the bands have since proven themselves capable of carrying out their new responsibilities.

Despite their success, the majority of Indian leaders across Canada oppose the agreements. They say both pieces of legislation imposed liberal democracy on the Indian communities. The traditions and customs of the Sechelt and the Cree were ignored. The powers now exercised by the Sechelt and the James Bay Indians were delegated by Ottawa and the provinces. The legislation reinforces the view that Indian governments are the tools of Ottawa and the provinces, administering only those functions that the senior levels of government have allocated to them. Such an act is a denial that those are rights Indian people should not have to bargain for. Ottawa has yet to state that either the Sechelt or the James Bay settlement should become the model for all Indian self-government aspirations, but it is clear that this is the only direction Ottawa is working towards and has been for almost two decades.

It was certainly the path recommended by the Nielsen Task Force. But it was also strikingly similar to the model the Liberal government of 1984 wanted to impose on Indian communities. Apparently having learned nothing from the White Paper fiasco of fifteen years earlier, the Liberal government moved unilaterally in 1984 with a piece of legislation called Bill C-52. Without native input, and completely dismissing a recent one-year study on self-government conducted by a special committee of the House of Commons, Ottawa came forward with a framework for all future Indian self-government settlements. The Liberal government was prepared to give an even broader range of powers to Indian communities than those granted by either the James Bay or the Sechelt legislation. This included the regulation of all land use, laws governing public order and control over the environment, including renewable and non-renewable resources, wildlife, and agriculture. The new policy even covered control over the administration of justice on Indian land. For the first time, Indians would be allowed to

establish judicial and quasi-judicial bodies with jurisdiction
over Indian laws, to create their own jails, to have Indian police
and prosecution authorities, and to set family law for all permanent residents affecting marriage, separation, divorce, adoption, and child welfare.

However, C-52 still subjected all Indian laws to Ottawa's
final approval and the Canadian Charter of Rights and
Freedoms. Predictably, the Indian community condemned the
legislation. They argued that Ottawa had only one concept of
government — a liberal democracy which had no room for
aboriginal customs and traditions. The legislation limited Indian jurisdiction to on-reserve residents. It remained silent,
however, on the right of any Indian authority to represent and
care for band members living in urban centres, which is a goal
of some Indian leaders. Indian communities would remain,
despite Ottawa's claims, mere instruments of the federal
government, carrying out only those functions assigned to it. Bill
C-52 died with the defeat of the Liberal government that year.

Much of the Indian opposition and reaction to Bill C-52
stemmed from the fact that their demands had been ignored and
their expectations for great gains had been raised only the year
before. In 1983, a special House of Commons committee,
chaired by Liberal MP Keith Penner, released a report strongly
urging Ottawa to entrench Indian self-government in the Constitution. The all-party committee had spent the previous year
holding hearings and reviewing submissions from native individuals and aboriginal organizations from across Canada. Its
recommendations were the first from a government body ad-
vocating recognition of Indian First Nations as a distinct level
of government instead of as mere municipal bodies with expanded powers created by Ottawa.

The Penner report urged Ottawa to entrench immediately in
the Constitution the right of Indians to self-government and to
pass legislation that would enable the Indian bands to achieve
that goal. As First Nations, the report said, bands have the right
to determine their own membership and powers, whether they
act alone or formally join other bands sharing the same traditions and language. The report concluded that various Indian

tribes were in fact nations of people who shared a common history and culture and language. And like the White Paper before it, Penner called for the dismantling of the Department of Indian Affairs. Their reasons, of course, came from divergent viewpoints. Where the White Paper's assimilation plans would make Indian Affairs redundant, Penner wanted it replaced with a smaller ministry to ensure that Canada's obligations to the distinct Indian First Nations would be maintained. A tribunal would be established to settle disputes between the emerging First Nations and other governments. A commission would be established to determine when bands were ready to assume their new status. And finally, the report recommended that Ottawa finance the new First Nations as it does the provincial governments with equalization payments.

## Moving Forward

The report insisted on liberal-democratic institutions as the basis of Indian government, ignoring native traditions and customs which date back thousands of years. It based Indian government on individual band councils, again circumventing any aboriginal attempts to re-establish traditions they had followed before the Europeans arrived. However, since the report allowed bands to determine their own future direction, there was some flexibility for band members to form a government more closely resembling their historical roots. The rights of non-status Indians and status Indians living in urban centres were again not addressed.

Even with its faults, Indian organizations applauded the recommendations of the Penner report. It was seen as a starting point for negotiations for a new arrangement between status Indians and Ottawa. Indian leaders believed the flaws could be overcome. Then a year later, with Bill C-52, Ottawa showed once again it was not listening. There was no suggestion that Ottawa would accept First Nations as a third and equal level of government, no hope for constitutional entrenchment which would legitimize aboriginal aspirations.

The refusal of Ottawa and the provinces to accept self-government has forced Indian groups to take a two-pronged approach in their struggle. The inherent right to govern themselves remains the objective. But they continue to assume more control of their own affairs by participating in Ottawa's devolution policy, while at the same time challenging the limits Ottawa and the provinces impose on them. The Sechelt and James Bay agreements are not what Indians want, but they are now using them to demonstrate to Canadians that they are capable of running their own affairs.

At the same time as well, Indians are turning with increasing frequency to the courts to gain ground that the provinces and Ottawa refuse to accede. Court cases in Manitoba and Nova Scotia, for example, have upheld Indian rights to hunt and fish regardless of provincial wildlife regulations, thus forcing the provinces into negotiations. Bands in Manitoba have over the past decade firmly established their own child welfare agencies on reserves but under provincial jurisdiction. Encouraged by other court wins, they have become the first to push for greater authority in the child welfare area by challenging provincial rights to restrict their activities to reserves only. Despite threats of court action, the Manitoba bands have moved to license foster homes and apprehend children in urban settings.

"Many Indian communities feel they've gone as far as they can in assuming control of their affairs from the federal government," says an adviser to native organizations. "They [Indian Affairs] have created a system of Indian institutions which are working but are still agents of the federal government. That was useful for a time because it allowed for the development of capabilities and institutions but it's no longer sufficient."

The cumulative effect of the court cases, the Penner report, and the demonstrated ability of Indian communities to succeed is being felt by Canadians. Provincial inquiries in Alberta, Manitoba, Ontario, and Nova Scotia have highlighted the inequities suffered by native people in white society. The Canadian Bar Association has called for the creation of a separate justice system controlled by native people. A national poll on attitudes towards aboriginal issues, conducted by the Angus Reid Group during the fall of 1989 for the *Winnipeg Free Press*, showed that 56 per cent of Canadians support the concept of aboriginal self-government. Canadians are now faced with a choice: continue the practice of the past 200 years and condemn the aboriginal community to further misery or offer Indians an opportunity to find themselves and their place within Canada.

# 5

# Economic Development

"Today there is the growing danger that a majority of Indians
... may become a more-or-less permanently isolated, displaced,
unemployed or under-employed and dependent group who can
find no useful or meaningful role in an increasingly complex
urban industrial economy."

Thus in 1966 Harry B. Hawthorn summed up his assessment
of Canada's first comprehensive review of Indian issues in this
one sentence. Hawthorn was the editor and director of *A Survey
of the Contemporary Indians of Canada*, the country's first
attempt to expose the widespread poverty and despair of native
people and to find an acceptable solution to integrate them into
Canadian society while still retaining their distinctive culture
and traditions. The study was commissioned in 1964 by the
Indian Affairs Branch (later to become its own department) of
the Ministry of Citizenship and Immigration. The study's findings and Hawthorn's own observation were a warning to the
government and people of Canada of what might happen to the
Indian community if actions were not taken to eliminate conditions that existed in the mid-1960s. The deplorable conditions on Indian reserves and for Indians in urban settings across
Canada exist today because of the failure of Ottawa's policies
to meet the challenge issued in the Hawthorn report.

Between 1968 and 1988, Ottawa spent more than $2 billion
on social assistance for Indian bands across Canada and almost

$2.5 billion on Indian economic development programs. With those expenditures, Ottawa created a national policy that pulled native people in opposite directions, with predictable results — they went nowhere. The 1986 census found that, on average, more than 66 per cent of Indians of working age were either unemployed or collecting welfare. On isolated reserves and in some urban centres, the figures reach as high as 80 to 90 per cent.

How could billions of dollars be spent with nothing more accomplished than the realization of Hawthorn's nightmare? The answer is not simple nor is there a single villain. Economic development was one of the few items specifically identified in the 1969 White Paper; the authors of this proposed new Indian policy set aside $50 million to launch native economic development initiatives. At the same time, Ottawa created a new ministry to reduce regional disparities across the country, the Department of Regional and Economic Expansion (DREE). A year later, the White Paper was officially withdrawn, and civil servants were told to direct their energies to DREE and the Hawthorn recommendations, which had been set aside until a new policy was drafted. Over the next twenty years, billions would be spent futilely, trying to fulfil Hawthorn's call to solve the depressed economic state of Canada's native community.

Many believe Ottawa's failure to succeed was rooted in the fact that no new policy direction ever evolved which might have ensured the long-term economic viability of Indian communities. "As political enthusiasm waned and new priorities came into vogue, Ottawa officialdom brought DREE 'into line,'" one federal official was quoted as saying in a consultant's report examining Ottawa's native economic policies. "Throughout, it has lacked clear, accepted goals and, increasingly, a coherent driving force." Devoid of any concise policy on where the government wanted to take native economic initiatives, programs evolved that simply handed social assistance to native people, stunting their economic development.

During the past two decades, economic development and the Indian vision of self-government have become inseparable and interdependent. Two hundred years of dependency devastated the aboriginal community. Now Indian leaders say real change can only be accomplished by ensuring that political changes and economic initiatives go hand in hand so that their people no longer remain dependent on white society.

A study in 1983 of seven Indian-run economic development agencies, conducted for the House of Commons committee on self-government (the Penner report), showed that Indian bands and their development arms believed that efforts by Ottawa to launch native economic initiatives had actually been counter-productive. Government programs proved to be too bureaucratic and time-consuming and not available for high-risk ventures. On reserves with little economic activity, every business venture becomes a high risk. Repeated assessments have concluded that government funding proved undependable and sporadic and actually hindered long-term development.

Analysis of federal studies obtained through the Access to Information Act not only confirm the Indian assumptions but also show that the programs were, in fact, destructive to many communities. A succession of key federal-provincial programs aimed at improving the economic viability of Indian reserves in western Canada did little more than build roads to lead Indians away from their homes. The studies which examine program effectiveness in Alberta, Saskatchewan, and Manitoba show that, although overall incomes and living standards have increased on reserves, the socioeconomic gap between native and non-native people has widened and more Indians than ever before are dependent on welfare. The repeated failures of the programs prompted one consultant to speculate that federal and provincial governments never intended to improve conditions for native people. The entire exercise was just an expensive public relations gesture. Ottawa and the provinces found it much easier to simply build things for Indians and were unable to lay the groundwork for a viable economy, which was one of the stated objectives and philosophies of the various programs.

It would be impossible to attempt an assessment of all the programs devoted to economic development during the past twenty years. Studies were obtained that examined what are commonly called northlands agreements, signed between

Ottawa and the three prairie provinces covering the period from 1974 to 1989. These have been chosen because they were promoted as innovative and successful by the federal and provincial governments, and because they have been in existence for many years. Independent assessments on them have been carried out.

## The Big Lie

The northlands agreements were initiated by the federal Department of Regional and Economic Expansion, which in later years became Regional Industrial Expansion. Total funding added up to more than $460 million. All the agreements were aimed at eradicating the disparities in the northern areas of the three provinces through the implementation of economic development strategies. Review of the independent studies show that all the programs, regardless of when or where they were introduced, failed to accomplish their goals.

As well, a look at the consultants' reports show that these government-funded analysts repeatedly glossed over their findings with a sugar-coated generalized introduction which often mislead the reader, before laying bare the real faults of the systems in a more detailed assessment. "Agreement represents a good application of public funds," noted the consultants who evaluated one of the three Saskatchewan agreements. They then went on to outline in great detail all the program's massive failings.

Between 1974 and 1989 Ottawa and Saskatchewan committed more than $212 million to three separate economic development initiatives. Assessments of the three, which make up the Canada/Saskatchewan Northlands Agreement, 1974-83, and the Northern Economic Development Subsidiary Agreement, 1984-89, show that the programs failed to improve conditions. Millions of dollars were spent on capital improvements, including housing, recreation centres, telephone systems, and roads, but there was no attempt to establish a local economy which would in turn lead the residents to some level of economic independence.

Reviews of the *Canada/Saskatchewan Northlands Agreement Evaluation* (December 1982) and the *Mid-term Review of the Canada-Saskatchewan Northern Economic Development Subsidiary Agreement* (1986) reached similar conclusions: despite the efforts and dollars, northern Saskatchewan suffers many of the same problems as a developing Third World country — a staggering population growth coupled with an absence of economic activity. At best, the agreements were able to provide training and jobs for a few people, but they proved totally inadequate for the great majority of the northern native population.

Provincial officials bypassed the co-ordinating components and long-term aims included in the agreements, and instead opted for what was easier to accomplish in the short-term, a massive construction campaign. Although this approach offered temporary economic relief to northern conditions, it made a mockery of the agreement's objectives of laying a foundation for real economic change in the north. "Unfortunately, other elements that make a community self-sustaining are still missing, including an economic base to provide permanent jobs for local residents and a tax base to operate and maintain the new facilities," the consultants wrote.

An evaluation of Saskatchewan's Northern Economic Development Subsidiary Agreement, covering the years 1984-89, show that the program had been a failure after two years and was destined to remain so. The program never met its objectives of economic planning, failed to create local jobs, and did not provide facilities for permanent employment. Although it did offer job-training, there were no jobs waiting for graduates. It appears to be another example in a long line of government programs that raised expectations only to deliver short-term opportunities.

This study also criticizes the federal and provincial governments' efforts to promote the agreement. Despite more than $25 million committed to the entire program, no efforts were made to publicize the availability of funds. This failure calls into question the motives of both governments. Did they really want to spend the money or was the entire program just a way to make southern residents think that something was being done? Statements made to the consultants by field staff and participants about the unavailability of funds support the view that there was little real commitment.

The study concludes that the multi-million-dollar agreement would have minimal impact on anyone. "There is no clear political priority placed on northern development by either federal or provincial governments," they wrote. "Given its scope and the very limited amount of 'new money' available to it, [the agreement] will never have more than a marginal impact in the context of all government programming aimed at economic and human resource development." And the litany of sins cited in Saskatchewan were being duplicated across the country.

The authors of another federally sponsored analysis, the *Canada/Alberta North Subsidiary Agreement Assessment*, paint a depressing picture of governments' efforts to improve northern Alberta native communities between 1975 and 1982. "One of the basic stated goals of the Alberta Government is to diversify and decentralize economic development in the province," the consultants noted. However, they said they could not see how this particular agreement and its programs could have lessened regional disparities in the north or disparities between northern and southern areas of the province.

In this case, more than $48 million was targeted to improve conditions in the northern communities but, just like its eastern neighbour, the Alberta government found it easier to spend on services and facilities, instead of launching a true local economy. Although this approach did improve some living conditions by constructing new housing and other facilities, the spending ended up working against the stated long-term objectives of the program. The study quotes a federal official: "You can spend as much money on hard services and infrastructure as possible. In this province it is a bottomless pit. With this particular project area [transportation agreement], it seems to be the emphasis of the [provincial] government to provide access roads to remote communities so that the residents can leave the community." Native and other observers have long suggested that a lack of real economic development has simply made it easier for native residents to take the new roads out and relocate in more established communities.

In Manitoba, analysts reviewing the Northlands Development Agreement, 1982-89, came to the same conclusions reached by the consultants in Saskatchewan and Alberta. Ottawa and Manitoba pumped more than $200 million into the northern part of the province during a seven-year period. In the end, only one thing had changed: more native residents were collecting welfare. Total welfare payments by Indian Affairs to reserve residents increased 30 per cent during the four-year period, from $20.5 million to $26.7 million. The analysts were left with the impression that the only people to benefit from the native programs were non-natives, southern Manitobans who moved north to take advantage of the construction activity.

## A Helping Hand

Government-subsidized ventures have been such abysmal failures that native groups have turned elsewhere to realize their economic development goals. The success rate of Indian entrepreneurs shows that, when left to manage their own affairs, they can and do thrive. The Quebec Cree own their own airline, Creebec Air. The Pas band in northern Manitoba is the area's second-largest employer and operates a successful multi-million-dollar shopping complex across the river from the non-native community of The Pas. Alberta Indians operate Peace Hills Trust, a trust company in western Canada. The Squamish Indians of British Columbia have turned lucrative landholdings adjacent to Vancouver into a multi-million-dollar operation. These are the ventures that Indian leaders point to as proof that, if given control of funds, they can avoid a life of welfare, as well as the misguided and wasteful programs Ottawa continues to implement.

Indian entrepreneurs have also increasingly turned to the private business sector for both funding and advice. And Canada's business community is slowly responding, having long ago concluded from their own experience that Ottawa lacks the expertise to implement its big-budget programs.

"I don't mean this in any negative way but government is highly expenditure oriented," Cliff Boland, president of the Canadian Council on Native Business, says. "What do they know about making profit, retaining earnings and re-investing back into the business?"

The council is a coalition of the country's top business leaders who say they feel obligated to help native people get started in business. Its supporters include the chairmen and chief executive officers of many of Canada's key businesses, including Northern Telecom, General Foods Inc., Brascan Canada, Cadillac-Fairview, Nova Corp, Xerox Canada, Shoppers Drug Mart, and IBM Canada. Started in 1984, the council has been quietly working with native entrepreneurs, offering advice and contacts but not money. It also operates an internship program which places native people with firms to learn business skills they can later apply to their own companies.

According to Boland, Ottawa's efforts have concentrated on short-term job creation and training projects but nothing long term. "Native people don't lack for the amount of government-oriented training. One of our success stories had gone to eight different training programs. She's one of the best educated people I've ever met. But she's never been shown how to set up a business or how to manage." Native people who want to go into business, he says, have no one to tell them how to get started and what mistakes to avoid. "We don't want to change their culture or tradition. We want to share with them our skills and our business network that they don't have."

A guilty conscience has prompted more than one business leader to join the council. "So long as we have this Third World in our own country, we have a soft underbelly in society that has to be addressed," says Don Noble, former executive vice-president of Northern Telecom and the council's past chairman. "On top of that, we all have deep down within us some feeling of a need to put something back and we're better [able] to do that with native people who've been too harshly disadvantaged over the years."

Ottawa has labelled most of the northern and isolated reserves as not economically viable and has targeted them only for

social assistance. Former Indian Affairs Minister Bill Mc-
Knight said in an 1988 interview that welfare must remain as
the safety net for Indians living in those areas. "What would
you suggest in an isolated locale, without markets, without
resources, without an industrial base, without economic opportunities? You try as best you can to provide a social safety net,
as we do to all Canadians." Such a statement seems to reject
alternatives that could lead to native self-sufficiency, at least
in the reserve setting.

Indian Affairs continually refuses to reconsider its spending
priorities when it comes to the country's 596 Indian reserves.
What Ottawa calls a safety net for the almost 274,000 people
who live on reserves, Indians call a crippling disease. Social
assistance has been a way of life for several generations and
has become a cycle which is almost impossible to break. "Our
welfare budget is $2.7 million and our economic development
budget from Indian Affairs is $52,000," says Louis Stevenson,
chief of the Peguis band and one of the Manitoba Indian
leaders. "If we had full control over those revenues, we could
reverse that arrangement where economic development is a
priority. Why couldn't we have $2.7 million at our disposal to
create jobs and to promote business and establish an economic
base on the reserve instead of pissing it down the drain on
welfare? You don't get a return on money from welfare. Once
that $2.7 million is issued, it's a one-way flow."

McKnight's negative attitudes towards reserves stem from
the frustration of years of failed cures. A broad spectrum of
Canadians who share McKnight's attitudes believe that reserves are nothing more than a drain on national resources. Others,
however, see these communities as opportunities waiting to be
tapped. Every native community needs an infrastructure of
grocery and hardware stores, repair shops, and clothing outlets,
but in most cases it has been supplied by white businesses.

The 1983 economic development study prepared for the
Penner report suspected that Ottawa believed most of the Indian projects would fail, leaving federal bureaucrats less than
enthusiastic about lending support and money for new
ventures. This places budding native entrepreneurs in a bind

because they need Ottawa's financing. The Indian Act prevents Indian land from being mortgaged, which in turn makes it impossible to mortgage a house sitting on that property. As a result, Indians have next to nothing to offer a lending institution as collateral for raising the kind of capital needed to launch a business. They need access to private capital to finance their ventures. Some favour the creation of an Indian bank which provides risk capital and investment experience. Toronto businessman Martin Connell has shown Ottawa and the Canadian business community that such a venture can work by starting his own bank, The Calmeadow Foundation, to support Indian ventures.

The gesture by Connell, president of Conwest Explorations Inc. and chairman of Toronto's Skydome, stems from a deeply held belief about sharing his good fortune with Canada's aboriginal people. The foundation, whose operating principles were borrowed from an experiment first carried out in Bangladesh fifteen years ago, works directly with individuals on reserves who want to start or expand a business. Five to seven people vouch for each other and form a loan circle. The first two get a loan, and if the payments are made, loans are given to the next two, and the process is repeated every two months. If someone misses a payment, the circle is broken and the loans stop. So far, Connell's experiment has proven successful. Working with three Ontario bands, the foundation made 116 loans, totalling more than $140,000, to 108 individuals since October 1987. Not one loan has fallen into arrears, and as of February 1990, sixty-four loans have been paid back in full. The loans ranged in size from $1,000 to $3,000, with $1,200 being the typical amount lent to Indian entrepreneurs. Two of the bands are located in remote areas, the Wikwemikong band on Manitoulin Island in Lake Huron and the Sachigo Lake band, located in northwestern Ontario near the Manitoba border. The third, the Kettle Point reserve, is located near Sarnia in southwestern Ontario.

Connell's approach could be one key to developing basic infrastructures on reserves. If reserve residents were to spend their money, either welfare or wages, on reserve businesses,

cash would stay inside and flow around the community, instead
of leaving the reserve or going to support non-native business.
Connell hopes to turn the foundation over to Indian control in
a few years.

## New Options

Indians living on reserves close to urban centres and those
living in major cities also see a potential waiting for development in set-aside contracts. For several years, Stan Fulham in
Winnipeg and Joe Miskokomon in Toronto have been busy
promoting this approach to native economic development,
which has already proved successful in the United States. It
simply involves the government stipulating that any contract it
awards to private industries must farm out part of the work to
native businesses.

"If General Motors is going to be making light tanks in
London [Ontario], then a certain amount of it has to be contracted out to light industry on reserves," says Miskokomon,
Grand Chief of the Union of Ontario Indians. He thinks Indians
on reserves can compete in the business world if they are given
help getting started. Ottawa and the provincial governments
must help bring the Indian community into the Canadian
mosaic, and according to Miskokomon, reserves should also be
seeking ways to act as suppliers for larger, well-established
industries in neighbouring urban communities. "The
economics of Indian communities is not big enough to sustain
business. You have to attract it. You either attract it into the
community or you manufacture something that will be
produced for someone outside in a bigger industry."

Fulham maintains that the set-aside contract model would
also work in cities where a mall or industrial park is owned and
operated by native entrepreneurs. Small businesses, such as a
barber shop or shoemaker, could survive alongside a larger,
anchor tenant. It would be the anchor tenant, something on the
scale of a supermarket or factory, that would become the
beneficiary of government contracts and ensure the financial
stability of the mall. "We can manufacture anything you can
think of ... salt and pepper shakers, pencils, whatever," says

Fulham, head of a non-profit native co-operative housing venture in Winnipeg and former secretary of the Manitoba Métis Federation. "The native community would have something they could identify with, but it wouldn't only be supported by native people. It would be supported by the community as well." Businesses in the mall would share costs and management skills to help each other succeed. "Basically what it is, is an incubator. You incubate small native businesses."

Twenty years ago Canada's Indian community embarked on a new path to regain complete control of their lives within a self-government framework. Tremendous strides have been made in local administration, child welfare, education, and housing. But economic development, the one area which was to have financed all the others, has suffered repeated setbacks while under Ottawa's guiding hand. Ottawa's ability to achieve only marginal improvements in the overall living conditions of the majority of Indian people has kept them trapped in Hawthorn's world of misery, poverty, and violence and has slowed progress in other areas. Worse still, the wasteful spending of billions of dollars on programs that were bound to fail has led many non-native Canadians to believe that it is time to stop any further spending and cast the Indian community off to fend for itself.

Despite all the obstacles Ottawa has thrown in their path, Indian entrepreneurs have at least a few success stories to hold up as models and as proof that they can survive and even prosper in the business world. And surprisingly, they are doing it with advice and financial support from the Canadian business community. Canada's business leaders, unlike many federal and provincial politicians and bureaucrats, have concluded that with proper and well-thought-out direction, real change can be effected within Indian communities.

# 6

# Health Care

For more than two decades, the federal government has said that it intends to bring the health of Canada's aboriginal people up to, or at least closer to, the general state of well-being enjoyed by most other Canadians. But all the evidence indicates that federal government expenditures in excess of $3 billion for Indian health care since the late 1960s, and all the accompanying bureaucratic and medical goodwill, have not been nearly enough. In 1961, the life expectancy of Canada's original people stood at sixty-one years, a full decade less than that of other Canadians. In 1981, that discrepancy remained exactly the same, with Canadians on average surviving until their seventy-sixth birthday and Indians only until their sixty-sixth.

Health studies and information provided by medical field workers throughout the 1960s paint a cold, clear picture. In the 1960s, native infant mortality rates stood at more than double the national average. Sexually transmitted diseases, accidental and violent deaths, alcohol abuse, and teen pregnancies were all serious health issues that the government had targeted for special attention. Tuberculosis, which was rare in the Canadian population as a whole at the time, and respiratory diseases were wreaking havoc in the impoverished native population. And on top of all that, non-competitive salaries and arduous working conditions were causing chronic nursing staff shortages, particularly for remote regions, leaving those in the field over-worked and frustrated.

Not much has changed in twenty years. Evidence in the 1980s shows that, though there has been some improvement in infant mortality rates and the incidence of diseases like tuber-culosis, which are linked to substandard living conditions, these rates still remain well above national averages. And even these few gains, note the experts, have all but been offset by setbacks elsewhere. In fact, health officials point out, the big-gest changes in the health of Canada's aboriginal people after twenty years of white medical intervention are the new health problems attacking them.

Violence, including suicides and accidents, remains the number one killer of Canada's original people. One study notes that, between 1974 and 1987, one quarter of all family-related murders in Canada involved native people. But the tragedy goes beyond violence. Cancer and cardiovascular disease, once rare among native people, are fast becoming the major killers. Diabetes, once unheard of among Indians, has now reached epidemic proportions in some communities, with levels more than three times the national average for people living off reserves. Sexually transmitted diseases continue to run out of control, with some estimates putting their incidence at ten times the Canadian average, raising fears in the medical profession about the devastating impact AIDS will have on remote com-munities once it is introduced. And, again, to top it all off, improvements in salaries and working conditions have failed to cure chronic nursing shortages, making the erratic delivery of programs almost a disease in itself.

More than ever before, say frustrated health officials throughout the country, native people are dying from diseases linked to self-destructive lifestyles, poverty-stricken environ-ments, and the legacy of the white society's ways. And, the medical experts argue, they are running out of answers because these diseases do not respond to medical intervention. The cure, they say, is beyond their jurisdiction. The answer lies in the political realm and in the wholesale acceptance of native self-government and control.

Indian health is a strange animal in the world of federal responsibility for Canada's aboriginal people. While Ottawa has for centuries accepted its legal liability based on treaty agreements for education, social services, and other basics, the question of who was responsible for the delivery of health services had been a sore point for decades and remained so in 1969 when the White Paper was introduced.

Health care is a provincial responsibility in Canada. But Indians have argued since the treaties were signed that it is Ottawa's job to oversee and pay for their health services. As proof, they point to Treaty 6, signed in 1867 between Canada and the Crees of what are now Alberta and Saskatchewan, which makes reference to the provision of a medicine chest "at the house of each Indian agent for the use and benefit of the Indians at the direction of the agent."

Ottawa has long argued that the provinces are ultimately responsible. But, on an interim basis, it accepted the burden of administrating Indian health on "moral grounds" because most provinces were ill-equipped to handle the complex needs of the residents of such remote communities. The Department of Indian Affairs handed over responsibility for the delivery of Indian health services to Health and Welfare Canada in 1945. A reorganization of field services in 1962 resulted in the creation of Health and Welfare's Medical Services Branch. The branch has served as native health overseer ever since and is responsible for the delivery of both treatment and public health programs in remote areas.

By 1969, little had changed. Federal authorities continued to espouse its long-standing policy of non-responsibility. "Despite popular misconception of the situation and vigorous assertions to the contrary, neither the federal nor any other government has any formal obligation to provide Indians or anyone else with free medical services," stated the 1969 Health and Welfare annual report. That view was reinforced that same year by then Native Affairs Minister John Munro speaking at a federal-provincial conference of health ministers. "There is no contract on health services between the Indians and the federal government," he said. And while Ottawa had delivered services "up to now," the government believed that, "where there are good facilities as there are in the southern parts of the provinces, the federal government felt that the provinces should be asked to assume the same responsibilities for Indians and non-Indians alike."

Ten years later a dramatic change would take place which, on the surface at least, appeared to set the administration of Indian health care on an entirely new path. Perhaps because of the complexity and scientific demands of the medical profession, or the fact that the smaller bureaucracy of the Medical Services Branch avoided the glare of centre stage during the mid-1960s and 1970s debates, the maturation of native health — specifically who controls the administration and related services — has lagged about a decade behind other native issues in Canada.

Like Indian Affairs, the Medical Services Branch has struggled with the daunting task of delivering services to a widely dispersed and diverse population. And, like Indian Affairs, the branch has for decades often responded to the multitude of practical problems — from chronic staff shortages to the sheer logistics of delivering services in the remote northern regions — with an almost arrogant self-confidence.

## A Litany of Sins

There is a plethora of research outlining a litany of sins, everything from the rejection of traditional Indian medicine to the removal of children needing medical treatment from their home communities for months and even years at a time. There is also some evidence that medical intervention throughout the 1970s bordered on the criminal. In 1977, for example, a Jesuit priest working with the Inuit on Holman Island questioned what he felt was a government program aimed at sterilizing Inuit women.

Aboriginal birth rates have long been an issue of study for medical experts. Until the mid-1940s, the Indian birth rate, both status and non-status, remained basically stable at about 40 births per 1,000 people. This number then began to climb until the 1960s and 1970s when it dropped from a high of 47 per

1,000 to 29, which still remained almost twice the rate for Canada as a whole. Medical experts point to a multitude of reasons for the sharp decline. Improved health services to the native population meant that women who wanted sterilization or needed hysterectomies because of problems related to multiple births and sexually transmitted diseases were more likely to receive that care. As well, the branch's educational programs had some impact on the use of birth control. But there were also indicators that at least part of the decline was the result of an overzealous pro-sterilization policy.

One medical expert in Manitoba described how he and his staff reacted in the mid-1970s when they first arrived in the north and found a thriving operating-room business. "When we got involved we were surprised to figure out how on earth some of those [operating rooms] were kept open two and three days a week in reasonably small communities," recalls Brian Postl, head of Manitoba's Northern Medical Unit which oversees the delivery of health care to remote native communities for the Medical Services Branch. "A very common procedure of those [operating rooms] was hysterectomies. No question. And we stopped that." Postl has said that, although he has never seen any data to prove that a written or unwritten sterilization policy existed among doctors or government, it is something medical experts heard, and continue to hear, rumours about. "Certainly, anecdotally, that's something we have all heard about and [it] probably did go on." And then there were all the smaller sins committed by a white medical profession trying to impose its will on a people who had survived for centuries without them.

As with all native issues in the 1980s, at the end of the decade the bureaucratic response to a lack of progress in native health care was to transfer power to Indian bands. The bureaucracy of the Medical Services Branch, once engrossed in providing health services and gathering statistics measuring disease and mortality rates, began in the late 1970s to focus instead on creating a complex, multi-stepped transfer plan to be adopted by Indian bands.

Like the equally complex issue of native justice, Indian health was not at centre stage when the White Paper was delivered in 1969. While the government's new philosophy would, of course, take in all aspects of native affairs, the departments of Indian Affairs and Health and Welfare went about their work as separate machines, with only a nodding acquaintance. In fact, the two departments communicated on mutual matters through an interdepartmental committee, a sore point for many who over the years complained that there were no clear lines of communication to help eliminate duplicated services or to ensure everyone was working on common goals.

And then there was the old question of federal versus provincial jurisdiction. But in 1979 the native-run Battlefords Indian Health Centre opened in Saskatchewan, and the jurisdictional question appeared to change when an official of the Medical Services Branch delivered a new federal policy, often referred to as "the Three Pillars." The Pillars policy is interesting for a number of reasons, not the least being the timing of the announcement. Unlike the Chrétien paper in 1969, there was no warning that the Medical Services Branch had anything in mind while the final touches were being planned for opening ceremonies of the Battlefords Centre. But on opening day, it became apparent that bureaucratic forces had been at work several thousand kilometres away when federal officials arrived armed with the new policy.

What the Three Pillars policy did was set a new direction for future native health services, while making a sudden, unwavering admission of federal responsibility. "Policy for federal programs for Indian people (of which the health policy is an aspect), flows from constitutional and statutory provisions, treaties and customary practice," began the third paragraph of the two-page document. "The Federal Government recognizes its legal and traditional responsibilities to Indians, and seeks to promote the ability of Indian communities to pursue their aspirations within the framework of Canadian institutions."

What a difference a decade makes. Only ten years earlier, the Medical Services Branch had reluctantly agreed to administer Indian health. Suddenly, in 1979, with Indian demands for more control growing across the country, the branch was admitting responsibility, and more. "The Federal Indian Health

Policy is based on the special relationship of the Indian people to the Federal Government, a relationship which both the Indian people and the Government are committed to preserving." This "special relationship," according to the policy's second pillar, would have to be strengthened by "opening up communication with the Indian people and by encouraging their greater involvement in planning, budgeting and delivery of health programs."

It would appear, at first glance, that the Medical Services Branch had done a complete about-face. However, a closer look at the three pillars shows that essentially little had changed. Despite the total rejection a decade earlier of Chrétien's White Paper and assurances to Indian leaders that those policies were not being quietly implemented, the Three Pillar announcement served notice that the federal bureaucracy was still working to have the provinces pick up a large piece of the administration of Indian services while the federal government would take on a new role.

Specifically, it was the third pillar that set out who would do what in the complex framework of the country's future Indian health care system. The federal responsibility was described as the "public health activities on reserves, health promotion, and the detection and mitigation of hazards to health in the environment." The provincial role was to be in the "diagnosis and treatment of acute and chronic disease and the rehabilitation of the sick." This was a major increase in the provinces' responsibilities, both financially and administratively. And native people, listed last and given the least to do, were to be responsible for the promotion of health and "adaptation of health services delivery to the specific needs of their community."

And then there was what the document called the most important pillar, the one that underwrote all other changes. In non-specific terms, the paper stated that health improvements must be built upon, first and foremost, "community development, both socioeconomic development and cultural and spiritual development to remove the conditions of poverty and apathy which prevents the members of the community from achieving a state of physical, mental and social well-being." It is a refrain that has been repeated for decades and one that is as much in vogue in 1989 as it was in 1979, or in 1969.

In August 1969, the health services consulting firm of Booz Allen Hamilton Canada Ltd., commissioned to study Indian health operations, released its report, which detailed for the first time the abhorrent conditions native people faced. The report's recommendations fell into two categories: short-term proposals dealing with the acute shortfalls in services and environmental conditions leading to disease and long-term proposals highlighting the need to change the socioeconomic conditions of Indian life. "To improve health services without making concurrent improvement in living conditions is analogous to treating the symptoms rather than the disease," stated the report. "In the long run, the provinces and Indians themselves should assume the responsibility for providing health services to Indians." The report envisioned the provinces taking over the major role in Indian health care within a decade.

In 1980, Justice Thomas Berger of the British Columbia Supreme Court headed a federal commission to study and make recommendations on Indian and Inuit health. "The matter of Indian health care is critical," wrote Berger in his final report. "The reason is that so many of the causes of Indian ill-health lie beyond the fact of the illness itself, and the remedies lie beyond the mandate of [Medical Services Branch]." He recommended, among other things, that a national conference on native health be convened. It never was.

"It has occurred to many folks here for a long time that we should stop counting the diseases the Indians are worse at, that we have reached the point of knowledge that we know they are in big trouble in terms of health," said Brian Postl of the Manitoba Northern Medical Unit in 1989. The unit, connected with the University of Manitoba, is contracted by the Medical Services Branch to provide health services to twenty-five northern Indian communities in the province. "We can get more and more specific and we can do more and more studies defining another disease that they have more trouble with, but at some point we have to take the step to link health status with socioeconomic conditions, social pathologies, alcohol and drug abuse. Health becomes an economic development issue." In northern Saskatchewan at the Battlefords Health Centre, director Alma King talks about the 80 per cent unemployment in the bands her centre serves, the alcoholism, and the federal government's approach to the problems. "I think Ottawa is more concerned with what its jurisdiction is and not getting involved in other things because it would be setting a precedent."

## Underlying Disease

There is more than ample evidence that this all-important pillar of the new policy never triggered the necessary massive federal initiatives needed to solve the underlying disease that ails Canada's native people. Instead, energies have been turned to transferring responsibility under the guise of self-governing initiatives. The sheer complexity of the transfer plan of the Medical Services Branch, as well as some of the negotiating tactics, indicate that the branch is mimicking several Indian Affairs' quirks as it moves to transfer control to Indians, characteristics native leaders have long used as evidence of a serious lack of good faith.

First of all, what the branch is transferring is a white bureaucratic system including all notions of decision-making and hierarchy and devoid of any native cultural component and little room to fit one in. Second, no new money is available despite an admission by the government that it will cost Indians more to run the same programs that the branch has struggled with so unsuccessfully for so many years. As well, despite the contradictions and inherent political infighting that has plagued the relationship for decades, Medical Services Branch has no thoughts of disappearing once transfer is accomplished. Like Indian Affairs throughout the 1970s, the branch's "special relationship" is being fostered for all it's worth. Cynics suggest that the 1979 Three Pillars policy was, in fact, little more than a thinly disguised manoeuvre to guarantee the branch's own survival by forging a new role in the midst of all the transfer hoopla. "Transfer does not mean goodbye," Health Minister Jake Epp told Indian delegates at a 1987 conference on health transfer in Montreal. "It means a new relationship between two partners, both equally dedicated to improving the health and quality of life of your people."

And then there is the issue of fear which has slowed things down as well. Like others before them, branch officials worry about everything from whether Indian leaders have enough expertise to control the show, to fears of political interference at the band level which could disrupt attempts to keep staff for long-term assignments, to whether programs deemed imperative would suffer or be dropped under Indian control. Thus, Indian bands looking at transfer proposals are faced with a barrage of rules, including spending restrictions, non-negotiable programs like immunization, and negative attitudes about everything from traditional medicine to home births. At the end of the 1980s, they are caught in what the Medical Services Branch calls its "pre-transfer stage" in which bands are given funding to prepare a feasibility study on taking over health care services.

During the 1987 National Indian Health Transfer Conference, organized by the Assembly of First Nations, Health Minister Jake Epp talked about the problems plaguing the transfer process. While he noted that bands and tribal councils were managing 25 per cent of the national Indian health services budget in 1987, he admitted that the restrictions on how the money could be spent and on what programs could be offered were causing many problems.

Epp's remarks echoed evidence given to a 1982 parliamentary committee, chaired by Liberal MP Keith Penner. As in other instances with Indian Affairs, native leaders complained that transfer was an illusion. "Indian witnesses were quick to point out that the devolution of health programs did not include transfer of control," reported Penner. "Real power remained with Health and Welfare." The leaders referred to Epp's vision of the branch's role after transfer. Based on the view that Parliament is ultimately accountable for tax money, Epp said that in its new role the branch would serve as watchdog, ensuring that money was being spent according to the transfer agreement by reviewing annual financial and community planning reports. As well, branch staff would serve as technical and teaching advisers for the bands.

But Indian leaders have argued that, if transfer is truly being conducted under the self-government notion, then both what is being transferred and how it is being done are so restrictive as to guarantee failure. First, only mandated programs are being offered, with no chance of moving funds from one program to another. Secondly, services that might offer some surplus funds from one year to the next because of effective preventative programming or simple underutilization, such as the dental and transportation services, are being tendered out to private contractors and are not on the transfer block. As well, no new money is being made available, despite the fact Epp admitted it will cost Indians more to administer the same services Health and Welfare has been struggling to handle on limited resources for decades, and that once they accept responsibilities, Indian bands will be solely responsible for any deficits they incur.

It is within this context that bands view the issue of power transfer. Some are opting for transfer despite the problems, believing that control, even of a troubled, underfinanced bureaucracy, is better than not being in the driver's seat at all. Others, however, reject what they see as too little money and limited control. These bands say they will not become the "administrators of our own misery." They argue that this transfer hoopla is the same trap Indian Affairs has set in its transfer initiatives in other fields — an intricate plot to renege on the federal government's responsibility as legal trustee and the accompanying financial burdens in a time of increasing fiscal restraint by shifting the responsibility onto the shoulders of provincial governments and Indians themselves.

Some believe that Battlefords and a handful of bands that wrestled a degree of control in the late 1970s and early 1980s, long before transfer became the *cause célèbre* of the federal government, are the lucky ones. "There wasn't a whole heap of planning," said Charlotte Johnson, a Manitoba director of the Medical Services Branch, about a dozen bands who ventured into the control quagmire in the 1970s. "I'm not sure anyone knew what the consequences were. And there were certainly people working on this side of government whose attitude was let's transfer. It's their problem now. There were a lot of growing pains, but I think the programs, by and large, have come out in ten years time to be pretty decent."

The bands that have taken control of health care may have been hampered by a certain naiveté about what they were getting into, say the envious ones, but they were not hindered by a massive bureaucracy focused on exactly what and how much was being given up. Certainly, the Battlefords Indian Health Centre and the few others like it offer some insight into what happens when the federal government finally cuts the strings and allows Indians to find their own way.

The Battlefords Centre began with a simple philosophy — to provide culturally appropriate programs to native people. The original directors made an early decision to concentrate on preventative programming and not on the provision of clinical services since they did not at the time have the expertise at hand. Spending of the centre's $1.5 million annual budget is directed by the chiefs of the eight Saskatchewan bands who gather for monthly board meetings in the two-storey modern cement structure located in the seedy part of North Battleford, Saskatchewan. "We don't have a lot of dealings with Medical Services or the federal government," explained Battlefords Indian Health Centre director Alma King. "We're funded by them. But our formal relationship is that we don't report on detailed program activities except for an annual report. And we provide monthly financial reports to them."

## Active Advocates

Several things have become apparent after more than a decade of operation. First, and foremost, staff believe they can respond to the needs of their communities more effectively than the decentralized Medical Services bureaucracy ever could. The centre is also living proof that the board's fears about pet programs or staff instability or even program deterioration were groundless. For example, once educated on such things as the need for immunization, band chiefs became active advocates on their reserves, say Battlefords staff. "Native people are often very scared of different pills and needles," said Larry Wuttunee, chief of the Red Pheasant band and chairman of the centre's all-chief health board. "We didn't know what they were before. Now the CHR [community health representative who is usually native] and the nurse will clearly explain."

Because all the centre's staff from nurses to Community Health Representatives are interviewed and hired by the board of chiefs and the programs are designed with input from the band chiefs, mutual respect for personnel and programs has developed. This makes employment far more stable than it ever was under federal direction. The vast majority of staff, 70 per cent of whom are native, have been with the centre from the beginning. "Our people [the centre's staff] have empathy for Indian people," said Jonas Semaganis, chief of the Little Pine band. "That's what makes us unique from other services."

The Battlefords Centre has also found that its separation from the Ottawa bureaucracy has resulted in a more holistic approach to health, one that often finds staff responding not only to the acute needs of its clientele, but also to some of the underlying causes of native health problems. "If someone comes in off the street for treatment and mentions they are looking for a job but have no resumé, we take the time out and help them write a resumé," says Joanne Lucarz, the centre's community health director. "That's going to make them healthier. What we try to do here is never say no, that's not our area. And none of the staff say that. That is what is different about Indian organizations. One Indian person will not say to another, 'No, that's not my job.'"

The centre also plays a liaison role with the white medical establishment. It has an employee who helps smooth interactions between native patients and Battleford-area hospitals. Lucarz, who often finds herself in the role, says the liaison person is called on to do everything from translating a doctor's orders into Cree to explaining traditional native medicine to often impatient and disrespectful hospital staff.

Although King and Lucarz believe the centre has successfully carved out its niche, there are fears that, if the federal government continues to pay only lip service to the underlying causes of native ill health, the sheer weight of the assignment will destroy the Battlefords Centre and others like it across the country. Lucarz has been told recently by federal officials that, if they had been in power in the 1970s, the centre would not exist. "When you say the feds want Battlefords-type centres to happen, I disagree," Lucarz says. "They don't want a powerful organization like this developing in too many places. Because it is really easy to pick off a band, band by band, but it is really hard to pick off eight bands."

And despite the inroads the centre has made in ten years, there are no illusions among the staff that they have cured what ails Indian people. Alcoholism, chronic unemployment, violence, diabetes, and other diseases continue to plague native people here as they do elsewhere in the country. But there are no statistics in Ottawa to support this. "In the first years, I was collecting a lot of good stats, but the other zones weren't," explains Lucarz. "We looked real bad. So we stopped counting."

So the native health care debate rages on, as Brian Postl and other professionals in the field continue their day-to-day fight against disease in native communities. And they wait with hopes for major changes. They see examples of successful native-run centres across the country. They see a slow movement towards self-government and the native people's sense of pride in their cultural heritage. And they watch the reluctant bureaucrats and the apathetic Canadians who allow things to continue as they have in the past.

"It is entirely in the political purview," Postl argues. "We can talk specific disease rates and death rates, but the bottom line ends up being a Cabinet decision. Whether or not to make the commitment to provide every Indian house on a reserve with running water and waste disposal. Whether or not to allow the economic development of some of these communities to proceed.... If you look at the areas that are most open to intervention or prevention, you're looking at injuries, accidents, alcohol, violence. Those are all issues of social structure chaos, and social economic development. If we did nothing else but look at those particular areas, we could do more for the health of native people than by almost any other function."

Hope for some backing on the native health care issue from the Canadian Medical Association, similar to the endorsement given by the Canadian Bar Association for a separate native justice system, is also years away, according to Brian Postl. Unlike the legal profession, which comes face to face in the courts with the failure to take action, only those health professionals directly involved with Indians can clearly grasp the issue, he explains. "I wouldn't say the Canadian Medical Association is unaware. But most folks don't spend much of their time dealing with or being involved with issues relating to Indian health."

Despite the warnings and worries about the future, there is still reason for some optimism. "Indian people are becoming more assertive in vocalizing what their needs are," Alma King maintains. "I think they are becoming more vocal about telling professionals what their needs are instead of being told that this is good for you."

"I think their self-destructive tendencies are turning around," explains Rita Dozis, a retired Medical Services Branch nurse with twenty-nine years of experience both within the bureaucracy and on Ontario and Manitoba reserves. "I think Indians are starting to realize they are the only ones who can stop it. But it will take a long time and that's something we modern whites don't have much of. When you stop and think that from the time we reached this country to the time we reduced them to nothing, it took over 200 years. Why do we think they have to recover in ten?"

Brian Postl also believes that the final solution rests with the initiative and energy of the native people themselves. "This is all a very large political issue that the general public doesn't sense is important enough to force action. And until that happens, I think politicians will do enough to make sure that there's nothing of huge embarrassment or scandal. It is really left to the Indian people and their lobbies to influence decisions, and I think they are getting really good at that."

The one thing that frustrates Postl, however, is the way Canadians continue to act as if the native problems weren't there. They can focus in unison on injustices elsewhere in the world, he argues, but can somehow ignore their lack of knowledge and concern about injustices facing their country's indigenous people. "If there's despondency, it is that our society as a whole, despite having a huge social system of mores, doesn't trigger into Indian people. Now, is that racism? I think it has to be. It is an ugly word, but it may be. It is a racism of omission."

# 7

# Education

For the staff at Indian Affairs, the days of spring and summer of 1989 were unlike any they had seen before. Starting in early March, Indian protestors began occupying every available space in the corridors and reception areas of department offices across the country, forcing department employees to step around and over them. In a matter of days, the situation escalated into the largest, peaceful Indian demonstration in more than twenty years. As the number of protestors increased, the bureaucracy ground to a halt. To keep government functioning, the police were called in, and hundreds of protestors were arrested in Winnipeg and Thunder Bay. In response, several started hunger strikes. In April, hundreds more, beating drums and bearing placards, gathered at Parliament Hill. In May, the Catholic bishops threw their support behind the native demonstrators.

The cause of the disturbance was a decision by then Minister of Indian Affairs Pierre Cadieux to place a cap on the department's post-secondary education budget, limiting spending to $130 million annually. The Indian community was furious. Just as native children were finally, though in small numbers, taking advantage of all available educational tools, Ottawa was trying to restrict the number of students attending university and college. In keeping with its devolution policy, Ottawa gave band councils the unpopular task of determining which students would receive funding and which would have to seek provincial student loans (more likely, these students would abandon post-secondary education). Of course, Ottawa's decision did not take into account the thousands of Indians living in urban centres who had no band council they could approach for funding. With this decision, Indian Affairs violated its own objectives of increasing the number of Indian students attending post-secondary institutions.

For the Indian community, Cadieux's decision was another example of Ottawa trying to frustrate native progress. Aboriginal people have been slowly recovering from the devastation caused by 100 years of white-controlled educational programs, which systematically eliminated their language and culture and ignored their place in history. Having gained control of many of their own grade schools and high schools, in 1989 Indian leaders realized the importance higher education would play in reviving their communities. Cadieux's move was a slap in the face to their demands for greater self-determination. They had no choice but to take to the streets to vent their anger and to plead their case before the Canadian public. At stake was what Indians believe is an integral component to their future — unrestricted access to post-secondary education. In the past, reaching university, never mind graduating, had seemed an impossible target for native people. Finishing grade school was often the best most could accomplish, and on some isolated reserves it still is.

In the twenty years since the release of the White Paper, Ottawa has spent more than $6.3 billion on native education, with little to show for it. Indian students continue to have higher dropout rates, poorer test scores, and more grade failures than national and provincial averages. The 1986 census reveals that 37 per cent of the adult Indian population was considered illiterate or had less than a Grade 9 education, which was almost double the national average; 5 per cent graduated from high school, compared to 13 per cent of all students nationally; and only 1 per cent were university graduates while 9 per cent of all Canadians held a university degree. Although there has been a gradual improvement in Indian education since the

1960s, the gulf between native and non-native students remains just as large. In twenty years, Ottawa's expenditures on native education produced nothing more than a generation of native students who were only slightly better educated than their parents.

How could a government spend billions of dollars with little real benefit? Indian leaders blamed a bureaucracy which insisted on hiring non-native teachers from urban centres to teach children who could not speak English. Some bureaucrats blamed the Indians. Others appeared blind to classroom reality; they were satisfied simply with the fact that education spending had increased.

The federal government's extremely poor record on native education has a long history. At the turn of the century, Ottawa lent its authority to missionaries who had been operating schools on some reserves by agreeing to fund the construction and operation of more schools. Amendments were passed to the Indian Act authorizing churches to take Indian children from their homes and parents and force them to attend the notorious residential schools. Church leaders, with Ottawa's support, took it upon themselves to "civilize" all the Indian children, to give them a "proper" Christian upbringing. For ten months of the year, native children were placed in what were essentially boarding schools where beatings were commonplace. They were forbidden to speak their native language and practise their traditional beliefs. Thus began one of the darkest periods in the relationship between Indians and non-native society.

Indian leaders believe Ottawa deliberately used the church institutions to destroy their culture. The incidence of abuse has been cited frequently and is too well recorded to be simply dismissed as isolated occurrences or the exaggerations of a few angry individuals. "I personally attended Indian Residential Schools for eleven years and on leaving it took me another eleven years to mentally undo the devastation perpetrated therein by religious and other fanatics," wrote William Clarence Thomas in 1982, a former superintendent of an Indian-run school board in Manitoba. "No one ever hugged us or told us they loved us. We were mere numbers. Strappings, beatings, hair cut to baldness, being tethered to the flag pole, half day school with unqualified tutors, and slave labour the other half were commonplace."

The devastation caused by the residential schools was widespread and long-lasting. Claims by Indians that the schools are at the root of many of their problems have been supported by clinical studies. Peter Hudson, director of the University of Manitoba School of Social Work, ties most of the emotional and psychological problems of the native communities — violence, drug and alcohol abuse, child abuse — to the residential schools. "One of the biggest impacts of the residential school system is there are now three generations of kids who are now adults who didn't experience a close, normal family life. Where do we learn how to parent? In the family where we are raised. Yet three generations of kids were raised in institutions. What would they know about parents, family life?"

Hudson says that the trauma of the residential school experience was one of the factors that forced Indians to turn to self-destructive violence. "People in residential schools tell stories about scrubbing themselves for hours to remove their brown colour, of any trace of being Indian. The inward violence takes various forms. There are no taboos any more. Everything comes up for grabs. It could take the form of child sexual abuse, spousal abuse, alcoholism, delinquency, vandalism. The violence becomes all pervasive. I suggest the violence is there as a result of the thought process, as being thought of as worthless and having no pride in who you are and what you are. The violence follows from that."

## Nothing Changes

Demands from Indian leaders in the late 1940s prompted Ottawa to begin changing the residential school system. Formal agreements were made with individual school boards and provincial education departments for the integrated schooling of Indian and non-Indian children. A Special Joint Committee of the Senate and the House of Commons held sessions across the country between 1946 and 1948. The sessions became

forums for Indian leaders to articulate their displeasure with the
residential schools and to demand changes. The improvements
were marginal, however. Education remained white education
which failed to recognize Indians as human beings. And Indian
communities had little or no involvement in the white school
boards.

Oscar Lathlin, chief of The Pas band, says that, faced with
those obstacles, the children of his generation never had a
chance. "If you tell a child right from birth that he's no good,
that he's a drunk, that he's not able to hold onto a job, that he's
lazy, that he's a welfare bum, that he's just plain no good, and
you tell him that over and over and over again, by the time that
child becomes sixteen years old, he actually believes that he's
supposed to be lazy."

Lathlin is chief of The Pas band in Manitoba, the province's
most prosperous reserve. At forty-two, he's beaten the odds.
Lathlin graduated from high school, took one year of university, and spent some time working for Indian Affairs before
returning home and turning to band politics. He, like all Indian
leaders, believes education is one of the keys to his people's
future. And for education to benefit his people, Lathlin says
Indians must take control.

As part of its reaction to the White Paper of 1969, the Indian
community pressed Ottawa to transfer control of education into
native hands. In 1972, the National Indian Brotherhood
presented its paper *Indian Control of Education* to then Indian
Affairs Minister Jean Chrétien. And, in keeping with Ottawa's
devolution policy on native affairs, he promised to give Indians
what they wanted.

In a speech to provincial education ministers in Regina on
June 23, 1972, Chrétien said that control of curriculum, teaching staff, and parental involvement would be key to the
department's devolution policy: "When Indian parents ask that
the curriculum recognize their cultural values and customs,
their language and their contribution to mankind, do not make
a mistake, they are not asking for the moon. Their request is
legitimate and reasonable." The new approach, he maintained,
would ensure that adequate funds would be provided to

upgrade facilities, that teachers would have proper cultural training and continued support, and that culturally relevant material would be added to the classroom curriculum. "Unless we make such provision," he said, "we can expect nothing more in the next twenty years than we have reaped during the past twenty years."

Twenty years have now almost passed, and today Indian control of native education amounts to nothing more than buying a service approved by Ottawa and the provinces. "Ottawa sets the formulas, they set the [funding] guidelines," says Joe Miskokomon, Grand Chief of the Union of Ontario Indians. "The province sets all the curriculum and Indian people write all the pay cheques and that's about the extent of [our] involvement in education."

A real transfer of power would give Indians more than the right to sign a pay cheque. It would give them the right to hire administrators and staff, set budgets, and incorporate native curriculum — powers every non-native parent already has through school boards. "We're not talking about reducing the quality of education but enriching it by putting in cultural components that we feel are important, like our language," Miskokomon says. "We're not talking about eliminating the sciences, the maths, and English. The [Indian] people who are going to compete in the world have to have those things but, at the same time, they shouldn't lose where they've come from. They should have the understanding and the foundation of where they've come from and why they are here."

On a superficial level, Ottawa has followed through on its policy of transferring control, at least by its own definition. There are more than 82,000 status Indians in schools across Canada, with 26 per cent attending 243 band-managed schools, another 25 per cent attending federal schools on reserves (a dwindling number as transfers to Indians occur on a yearly basis), and the remainder attending provincial schools. Indian control has been delegated to almost half of the country's bands, who have either kept it or passed it on to native education authorities. Most often, these authorities operate like school boards with elected representatives from the reserves.

In theory, the authorities are responsible for hiring academic and support staff, co-ordinating curricula, and drafting budgets. Yet, in reality, the extent of their control is determined by Ottawa's willingness to support them.

## Bound by Purse Strings

Indians complain that their ability to direct their own education is severely curtailed because of legislative inadequacies and lack of funding. Policy in this area, as in others, has been ad hoc. Sections 114 to 123 of the Indian Act give the Department of Indian Affairs the authority to operate schools and enter agreements with provinces and territories to provide for education on reserves only. All other decisions have no legislative support. Ottawa has no legislative right to allow for the creation of Indian education authorities. There is no national Indian education act. Academic standards are set by each province. The entire framework of Indian education has been created by Cabinet orders and Treasury Board guidelines. Without a legislative framework detailing what the federal government's education obligations are, Ottawa provides only what it deems necessary. Policies covering everything from the creation of kindergarten classes to devolution, and those that allow Indian education authorities to exist, are set by the government of the day and bureaucrats. And policy, as the Indian leadership has discovered, changes with public opinion and partisan political priorities.

The Indian school authorities depend on the generosity of Ottawa. They have no alternate means to raise funds for their budgets. Unlike non-native school boards, they cannot levy taxes against the residents on their reserves. Bingos often help recreational programs but nothing else.

Education spending has always been Indian Affairs's single largest item, but the well has been drying up. Annual spending went from $70 million in 1968 to $433.6 million in 1982-83, but the budget has been fluctuating ever since. It peaked in 1986-87 at $539 million, then dropped to $476 million by 1988-89, and started to rise again the following year with a budget of $487.7 million. Indian authorities complain that long-term planning is impossible because they have no idea how much money will be made available from year to year. And the money that does arrive often arrives late, which forces authorities and bands to borrow funds while they wait, thus incurring interest charges which Ottawa never makes up.

The budget uncertainty is occurring at a time when Indian student enrolment is expanding greatly. In 1975, there were almost 72,000 Indian students attending on-reserve schools. Ten years later, there were more than 82,000 students in classrooms. Now Indian leaders say they need more funds to develop culturally relevant classes and offer teachers cultural training, but the dollars are not there. Statistics and studies show that the money spent in the past was never enough and that it was badly managed because native leaders lacked experience. Now that the Indian leadership has acquired the experience to manage its own affairs, Ottawa will not provide the money necessary to give individuals the training they need in the education field.

The federal government's devolution experiment in Indian education produced no better results than the residential schools had. Its failure has been documented several times, mostly by its own staff. In 1978, Indian Affairs released *Education of Indians in Federal and Provincial Schools in Manitoba, Evaluation Report*, which analysed school records of Indian students for the previous four years in the federally supported reserve schools and in those operated by the province's Frontier School Division. It concluded that there was little difference between the performance of Indian students in either system: there was a high dropout rate; 30 per cent of students were behind at least one grade; very few graduated from high school; absenteeism was common; and there was little parental involvement. As is typical of Indian Affairs, nothing was done.

Four years later, the department released a scathing internal report which clearly put the blame for the poor academic record of the Indian students on the shoulders of the bureaucrats. According to the *Indian Education Paper, Phase 1*, Ottawa's policy of transferring control of education had been flawed since Chrétien's announcement ten years earlier. What Ottawa had done — and what Indians have always maintained — was simply transfer control of a badly flawed program to people who were not trained to administer the system as it was and who lacked experience to correct its failings. "This policy emphasized both the need to improve the quality of Indian education and the desirability of devolving control of education to Indian society," the *Indian Education Paper* states. "The problems which now face Indian education were all either existing in 1973 or can be traced back to inadequate policy definition and inadequate devolution preparation and procedures."

The paper clearly details what was wrong with the department's policy. In the name of devolution, Ottawa reduced its support for curriculum development, teacher and student support, and monitoring of standards. Indian education authorities were not given the support necessary to deliver a quality program. Flaws in the federal system remained with the transfer. No one had defined "Indian control." Among the flaws transferred to Indians were an irrelevant curriculum which did not reflect an Indian child's history or circumstances, inferior school facilities, and an education staff characterized by high turnover, inadequate training, and low morale — everything that Chrétien had promised to solve.

Ottawa did very little following the release of its *Indian Education Paper* in 1982. In an interview, John Rayner, assistant deputy minister of Indian Affairs, said that the department wanted to hear, once again, from the Indian community before it took any corrective action. That Indian response would not come for another six years. To avoid implementing changes, Ottawa deftly bought that time by funding a multi-million-dollar study launched by the Assembly of First Nations, the national lobby of Indian bands formed in 1981. The Assembly surveyed all band leaders to find out what was wrong with the existing system and how they wanted to change it.

In the spring of 1988, the Assembly repeated what Indian people had said sixteen years earlier in the National Indian Brotherhood paper. Its three-volume report, *Tradition and Education: Towards A Vision of Our Future*, states that education programs in federal and provincial schools were irrelevant because they refused to acknowledge aboriginal languages, culture, and spiritual beliefs. The paper calls for education to become a cornerstone of self-government — constitutionally entrenched — and for aboriginal languages to be given official status. "Education, as a force in human development, lies at the base of achieving effective self-government," the paper's authors wrote. "Self-knowledge, self-confidence, self-respect, and self-sufficiency must be developed in order for any people to attain a healthy society, a stable culture, and self-government."

The paper reveals that there is no unanimity among Indian people on all the details — whether the language of instruction should be English, French, or native; or whether teaching staff should be all native, all non-native, or a mix of both. But it concludes that each band has the right to answer those questions on its own and within a time-frame of its own choosing. "People are saying we want to have control of our lives, our own children, to direct our own future," Joe Miskokomon adds.

The paper calls for Ottawa to give up its administrative and policy functions and remain only as a funding agency. Instead of adapting various provincial curricula to include native culture, the paper calls for an integration of the two, leaving the flexibility needed for individual bands or organizations to develop a program that meets their people's goals and objectives. Instead of inserting a daily class on native culture, Indian leaders want to start from the beginning, ensuring that all the lessons reflect traditional customs. "Learning must be associated with spiritual, physical, and emotional growth, as well as academic growth," the paper states. "Traditional First Nations methodology of teaching and learning must be considered. It is imperative that First Nations use the strategy of placing *education into culture* rather than continuing the practice of placing *culture into education*."

The federal government's response to the paper has been more delay to avoid having to make any real changes. Despite the presentation of two major policy papers from Indian organizations and its own studies during the past twenty years,

Ottawa pretends it needs more time to develop the appropriate strategy. Meanwhile, it continues its policy of administration by bureaucracy. Rayner says Indian Affairs is developing another policy position on education to address the issues identified by the Assembly of First Nations paper but gave no time when that policy would be produced. "We're working on an overall document on objectives and policy. We have to be sensitive to the needs of Indian people. It's their education. If they don't buy into it, we can't deliver it."

The inadequacies of the present education system go far beyond Ottawa's direct delaying tactics and blundering on policy; they are also shaped by the realities of the day. Many reserves offer a bleak existence to their residents, whose connections to the affluent outside world is often through satellite television and occasional trips to urban centres. There is also a built-in suspicion among many Indians who have experienced the negativism of the education system and are now unwilling to offer encouragement to their children despite well-meaning promises.

Sandy Lindsay, a retired superintendent with the education branch of Indian Affairs, says Indian parents have to shoulder some of the blame for their children's poor academic performances. "Maybe parents feel that school isn't meeting any of their basic needs. The three R's are still the total program today. [Schools] are preparing students for university and jobs in the technological south, yet they're living in the community where there are none of the jobs available based on the kinds of training they are getting, and they have no intention of leaving."

On a desk in the basement rec room of Lindsay's home is a stack of course studies he prepared for northern native schools. While still with the department, he found that many students knew very little about their surroundings, about the wildlife and vegetation. His courses would have taught the students what their parents may have forgotten, but the department never approved their use. Bureaucrats decided that an education program designed for a student in Toronto was adequate for an Indian child. Lindsay says that kind of program of education, coupled with the Indian child's perception of the outside world, creates unrealistic attitudes. "Our surveys indicated kids want to stay in the north, but they want inside jobs where it's warm and comfortable, a desk job, and they expect the kinds of wages that would give them a good living without hunting or fishing."

According to a principal of a northern Manitoba band school, despite the efforts to establish a more culturally relevant curriculum, expand language instruction, and hire native teachers aides, academic performances remain poor. "Up to Grade 6, attendance is very good. After Grade 7, attendance drops off. When the older kids hit Grade 7, they stay up all night shooting pool. There are four pool halls [on a reserve with a population of slightly more than 1,000]. If they come in at all, they sleep at their desks. We tried almost everything to encourage attendance, including giving out prizes and cash awards." In 1988, the band council provided $5,000 in gifts and cash to reward students (bicycles, televisions, stereos, and $20 gift certificates were handed out for best academic records and $10 gift certificates for best improved records). It didn't help.

"Part of the problem is the lack of support from the families. Parents encourage children only up to the grade they reached. After that they don't care," the principal says. "The biggest problem is alcohol. It affects both the parents and children. The reserve went dry two years ago, but the problems are worse now. We offer counselling for drug, alcohol, and sex abuse, and if we could get rid of the alcohol, we'd get rid of a lot of problems." According to Lindsay, the problems encountered by this school principal can be overcome with community leadership. Indian leaders cite several examples where parent involvement and encouragement have boosted attendance records to levels comparable to non-native urban schools.

Ottawa has signed agreements with the provinces to send Indian students to provincial schools, usually for the high school grades. These schools are often located in rural areas. But provincial authorities and Indian leaders have found it difficult to convince children to leave their reserves for higher education. Indian students are intimidated by the world beyond their reserves, which partly accounts for a high dropout rate.

The 1986 census shows that almost 40 per cent of Indians drop out before Grade 9 and only 5 per cent finish high school. Many of these students come from poor families who cannot afford to spend money on such things as trendy clothes. Others find the racist attitudes of their non-native classmates disturbing.

"We're talking about proud people," says Konrad Sioui, Chief of the Secretariat of First Nations of Quebec. "They don't want to go to school to be laughed at because they look too poor. Our kids are no different than others. They all want to succeed, but when they get into these melting-pot schools, the children are pushed away, treated as second-class citizens, discriminated against, sometimes even by their own teachers." Those not strong enough to stand up to the pressure, Sioui says, retreat back to the reserve. "They say, 'If that's the way I'm treated outside, why should I go, try to do my best?' Inside the reserve it might be poor, but at least we're able to have some relations and respect between ourselves and that is sufficient for me."

Most of the children who do stay in school go elsewhere to find a job. "That's one of the tragedies," says a provincial school official. "The communities need as many qualified people as they can get. The sad part of it is, because there's such high unemployment, young people will set their sights somewhere else." But Chief Oscar Lathlin thinks that keeping the children in school is all that is important, even if they decide to work off reserve when they graduate. "I don't care whether those university graduates come back to the reserve. What I care about is now they're in the position to make some choices."

## A Future Threatened
When former Indian Affairs Minister Pierre Cadieux announced in March 1989 that Ottawa would cap post-secondary education spending, in typical federal fashion, it was done without Indian consultation. More importantly, Indians considered it a violation of their treaty rights. Indians have always broadly interpreted the education rights given to them under the treaties, while Ottawa has held a narrow and literal reading. Indians say education means from kindergarten to university.

Ottawa says it is bound only to provide primary, elementary, and secondary schools on reserves; anything beyond that, it does through its own generosity.

"We know for sure that if you would interpret a treaty and you want to test it in any court, any judge would say, yes, post-secondary is included in that treaty," Konrad Sioui says. "You've got to adapt what is written in a treaty to what it means today, and any judge would do that. We've always said that education is a fundamental right. The treaties said that the Indian would be educated as the white man are."

Cadieux echoes government policy, a tactic used in many other areas when dealing with Indian issues. There was no mention of post-secondary education in the treaties, so Ottawa funds it at its pleasure. Cadieux's announcement also marked a reversal in Ottawa's commitment to increase native enrolment in post-secondary institutions. The department's 1985 report, *Post-secondary Education Assistance Evaluation Study, Final Report*, said one of the department's goals was to achieve a participation rate in post-secondary education at least equal to that of the non-native Canadian population. In 1969, Ottawa spent $250,000 on post-secondary education (in addition to spending for elementary and secondary education). Today, Ottawa spends $130 million. It's a phenomenal increase, but its real accomplishments have been meagre. Twenty years ago, native participation at this level was almost non-existent, while the national average was about 10 per cent. Today, the national enrolment at the university level is 20 per cent; native participation, according to the 1986 census, was 6 per cent. It was a gap that Ottawa promised to eliminate. A cap on spending could make it permanent.

Cadieux's decision highlights the two main concerns about Ottawa's ad hoc education policy: it is based on the whims of Cabinet and the funding is inadequate. In a letter to all chiefs and band councils dated March 20, 1989, Cadieux sent an ominous message: "The [post-secondary] program will have to live within its annual allocation which may mean that a small number of students will temporarily have to seek those sources of support available to other Canadians. The challenge now is to ensure that the substantial funds already in the program are used as effectively as possible to produce graduates with qualifications that will assist communities in moving towards self-government and improved economic growth."

Band councils, who administer the loans, are faced with a dilemma. They need the professionals to ensure their own growth and development, but Indian students may opt for a life outside of band politics and administration. Students who want to get into the band-controlled program must channel their interests to meet the goals of self-government and economic growth; only those with interests in becoming chartered accountants, lawyers, planners, and professionals need apply. For the others — those who want to study art, music, history, political science, languages — the only recourse is to apply to the provincial education departments for student loans.

The old guidelines gave Ottawa a good image at home and internationally. But that image will be tarnished as the old guidelines are changed simply because Indians are actually taking advantage of the program in numbers that Ottawa never expected, or was never prepared to fund. In 1969, there were less than 500 Indians attending university or college programs. By 1982, there were almost 7,000 student attending post-secondary classes. And by 1988, that number had more than doubled to over 15,000 students. "It was easy to put that old policy in place because there were very few of our people that would get a university degree," Sioui says. "So, in the eyes of the world, of the Canadian people, that looked very sharp. It was a very nice policy. Now that we're arriving at that stage, now that we have some chances to bring some of our people to the post-secondary level, Ottawa says we can't. Where is the rationale? Where is the logic?"

Sioui says the native demonstrations and sit-ins were an attempt to show Canadians what was at stake. "That policy is a threat to our youth that we will always reject. Just the fact that they would even talk about putting that in place unilaterally is a sign of how they want to treat us, how they want to keep us second-hand, not wanting us to get higher degrees and higher jobs and to become more self-sufficient."

Such a policy change supports observations that Ottawa will never support self-government and will continue, despite continued denials, to shift a greater burden of responsibility onto provincial governments. The only way to bridge the gap between native and non-native students enrolled in post-secondary programs (6 per cent versus 20 per cent) would be to more than triple the $130 million budget. With its change in policy, Ottawa is saying the provinces, and Indians themselves, will have to make up the difference.

Most Indians are unemployed, and only a small number have full-time jobs. Few would risk a loan without the security of a reserve or Indian organization job waiting for them after graduation. If an increasing number of Indians are forced to borrow to fund their education, the majority of them simply will not go. Without that education, they lose the freedom to choose how they want to live their lives.

Chief Oscar Lathlin says that only with a proper, Indian-controlled and -directed education system will Indian children regain the identity stolen from their parents and grandparents decades before. "The trick is to maintain your roots while getting an education. You can get your Masters in science or get a PhD or become an electrical engineer and still be an Indian. That's the kind of programming that we need but was never delivered by Ottawa."

With education comes the opportunity to exercise choice. "Before we had no choice," Lathlin says. "Whether we stayed on reserves and were dirt poor, living on welfare and actually believing that's our culture. Or we come to North Main. Or we go to jail. That's not much of a choice."

# 8

---

# Child Welfare

In no other area did federal bureaucrats and professional social workers wreak so much havoc in such a short period of time than in the field of child welfare. During a twenty-year period from the early 1960s to the early 1980s, many Indian communities across Canada lost an entire generation of children to the custody of provincial child welfare agencies. Professional workers, claiming to be acting in the best interests of the children, simply scooped them up and took them away. Parents never saw their children again. These children grew into troubled teens and adults — tortured by a past they could not reclaim, psychologically twisted from living in a world where they did not belong. Most of these children have turned to alcohol and drug abuse, many remain in psychiatric institutions and prisons, and many more chose suicide as their escape. It was a situation which Edwin C. Kimelman, associate chief judge of the Manitoba Family Court, accurately described in a 1985 report on native adoption and foster placements as the routine and systematic "cultural genocide" of Indian people.

When Ottawa, at the insistence of the Indian community, began phasing out the despised residential schools in the 1960s, children were returned to parents who were suffering from that same experience. Native family life had been destroyed by the residential school system. When their children were returned to their families, the parents were confused about their new parenting roles. They could not turn to their own parents because they too had been devastated by the same experience; they had no advice, nor were they models, for their children. These parents turned to alcohol and drug abuse to deal with their own hurt and, as a result, their children often became victims of physical and sexual abuse.

Ovide Mercredi, a vice-chief of the Assembly of First Nations, says Indian communities had their own support systems for child abuse before the massive intervention by non-native society. "In the past there had always been support in the community to look after families. If a parent or parents were neglecting or abusing their children, someone would come forward, not necessarily a chief, but someone they respected ... maybe an elder, a relative, a friend ... someone who would talk to them, tell them to straighten themselves out. If they didn't correct the situation, the chief or others would step in and remove the child from the family and place him with relatives or friends. The parents had no choice. Even if they objected, they could not get the child back until they turned themselves around."

In 1951, Ottawa amended the Indian Act to allow provincial agencies to extend child welfare services onto reserves but did not provide any funding to encourage the provinces to become actively involved. The result was a patchwork of service delivery across the country over the next thirty years. Although some provinces did provide limited services, others did nothing except to intervene in emergency situations.

With the loss of the traditional way of life, a growing dependency on welfare, and the placement of children in the care of their parents who often lacked the necessary emotional stability and skills, emergency situations quickly became the norm on reserves. Problems became so widespread that the traditional safeguards were overwhelmed. "They [native parents] turned to drinking and that led to other things," Mercredi says. "They became very irresponsible. They didn't look after their children. More than one family had the problem and the community could not respond."

With no support from Ottawa or the provinces, Indian society slowly crumbled. Indians became a people with lost or confused identities and a severely crippled sense of self-worth. Their only escape was an alcohol- and drug-induced numbness. The norms of acceptable social behaviour broke down. Over the years, it became a downward slide into oblivion. Indian agents and provincial social workers found the situation horrifying, but instead of trying to deal with the cause, their simple solution was to remove the children from their parents.

Writer Patrick Johnston, in his book *Native Children and the Child Welfare System*, coined the phrase "sixties scoop" to describe what happened during this period. In British Columbia in 1955, of the 3,433 children placed in protective care, less than 1 per cent (twenty-nine) were native. By 1964, native children represented 34.2 per cent (1,446 children) of the total 4,228 children in care. The passage of time only compounded the horror. In every province across Canada, native children in care were far more represented than their sheer numbers warranted. By 1980, almost 7,400 children, or 4.6 per cent of all registered Indian children, were in care across Canada, compared to less than 1 per cent (75,000) of all Canadian children. By 1985, the numbers had climbed higher; there were over 8,500 Indian children in care, representing 6.4 per cent of all status children, while the overall Canadian numbers remained at 1 per cent.

The situation was worse in Ontario and the four western provinces. In 1980 in British Columbia, native children accounted for 36.7 per cent of all children in care, but only made up 3.5 per cent of all children in the province; in Alberta, 29.7 per cent of all children in care, but only 2.9 per cent of all children; in Saskatchewan, 63.8 per cent of all children in care, but only 8.3 per cent of all children; in Manitoba, 32.1 per cent of all children in care, but only 7.7 per cent of all children; in Ontario, 8 per cent of all children in care, but only 1.1 per cent of all children.

For non-native children, being placed in care was usually a temporary situation. Not so for native children. The majority were either shuffled from one foster home to another for years or permanently adopted. Most never went home again. The majority of the foster home placements were with non-native families, and an Indian Affairs study of placements between 1971 and 1981 revealed that the great majority of Indian children who were adopted also went to non-native families. Many people believed these children would be better off removed from the poverty and life-threatening conditions on reserves, but time has shown that they went from one hell into another.

Carla Williams and Cameron Kerley are the two most publicized examples of Indian children taken from their families and placed in non-native homes. Both were born on Manitoba reserves and both were taken out of the country by adoptive parents, Cameron to Kansas and Carla to The Netherlands. Both were physically and sexually abused by their adoptive fathers, and both came home but under different circumstances.

Cameron was eight years old when his father was murdered. He and his three sisters were placed in foster homes by the Children's Aid Society. Their mother died two years later from heavy drinking. When Cameron was eleven, he was adopted by an American bachelor, Dick Kerley, and taken to Kansas. Soon after, Cameron became a problem child. He skipped school and ran away from home. He started drinking and doing drugs.

At nineteen, Cameron killed Dick Kerley with a baseball bat. He pleaded guilty to second-degree murder and in 1983 was given a life sentence. It was only then that Cameron told the world about his life with Dick Kerley — a horror story of physical and sexual abuse which he ended with the swing of a baseball bat. After serving two years in an American prison, Cameron went home in 1985 to serve the remainder of his twenty-year sentence in a Manitoba prison. He was eligible for full parole in May 1990.

Carla Williams's parents were Ojibway Indians from a southern Manitoba band who had moved to Winnipeg. They were alcoholics and their heavy drinking prompted the Children's Aid Society of Eastern Manitoba to seize their four children in 1968. Following the birth of their fifth child a year later, society officials seized him as well.

Carla was four years old in 1968 when she was placed with a non-native foster family. Three years later, her natural father hanged himself. In 1972, Carla was placed for permanent adoption with a Dutch couple who then moved back to The Netherlands. Even though the adoption broke down within a year and Carla was placed in a succession of foster homes, she could not escape her nightmare. Her adoptive father, a prominent physician, was given visitation rights and continued to sexually abuse her for the next seven years. She tried to kill herself at the age of twelve and was placed in a psychiatric institution. She remained under psychiatric care as an out-patient for the next three years, but even as an out-patient, the torment at her adoptive father's hands continued.

Carla became a mother at the age of fourteen, and the child was taken away from her. A year later, she had another child, and that one too was taken away. Both children were fathered by her adoptive father. She married at nineteen and became a prostitute. Carla had two more children, with two different men, and those also were taken away.

At the age of twenty-three, Carla encountered Canadians travelling in The Netherlands, a contact that led her to a Manitoba Indian child welfare agency, which re-united her with her native family. In the fall of 1989, at the age of twenty-five, Carla hugged her brothers and sisters at the Winnipeg International Airport. She had remarried, was pregnant with twins, and had developed what was expected to be a fatal disease. According to doctors, she could live for another six to eight years.

Following protests from Indian leaders, the Manitoba government stopped the out-of-province adoption of Indian children in 1982 and asked Judge Kimelman to examine the issue. Kimelman's report in 1985, *No Quiet Place*, was a comprehensive compilation. He concluded that the damage to Indian children was real and widespread.

Kimelman quoted the work of a Minneapolis doctor who had extensively studied Indian children who were raised in foster homes or adopted. His studies indicated that Indian children placed in white homes would, as teenagers, likely suffer emotional problems and turn to drug abuse and suicide. "All available information would indicate that the Indian people were correct in their assertions that once their children entered the child care system they were not likely to ever be returned to their own families," Kimelman wrote. "The evidence would indicate they were correct in their claim that not only were those children lost to their own communities, the lives of the individual children were seriously and permanently impaired."

By the late 1970s, Indians were becoming aware of the destructive nature of the non-native child welfare system. And, as part of their self-government aspirations, they demanded their own agencies, which would be administered and staffed by Indians and held accountable to their own people. That dream has been partly realized. Almost 4,000 Indian children, or 40 per cent of all Indian children in care in Canada, are now cared for by Indian-run agencies.

In all instances but one, these agencies have replaced the functions of the typical, non-native Children's Aid Society. They are staffed by Indian care workers, have Indian supervisors and directors, and are accountable to a board of directors chosen from the community or consisting of band council representatives. However, they remain under the jurisdiction of provincial legislation. Ottawa has refused to enact national Indian child welfare legislation, insisting that this area has always been the exclusive jurisdiction of the provinces. Agreements among Ottawa, the provinces, and the bands or tribal councils, which established the agencies, have always recognized the ultimate authority of provincial legislation. The agencies' right to apprehend children and offer protection and prevention services is mandated by provincial law, and the agencies remain ultimately accountable to a provincial authority.

The one exception is the child welfare program of the Spallumcheen band in British Columbia — the only Indian band that has succeeded in achieving complete autonomy in the area of child welfare. Like other agencies, it is funded through the

Department of Indian Affairs. Unlike all others, the Spallumcheen's agency was created by a band bylaw in 1979, which asserts its own jurisdiction and replaces that of the province of British Columbia.

The study of the Department of Indian Affairs, *Indian Child and Family Services in Canada, Final Report*, reviewed the agency's services from 1980 to 1986. It showed that the Spallumcheen program had reduced the number of children taken into care and, more importantly, had increased its reliance on extended family care. The federal study also concluded that the Spallumcheen had achieved far more than other bands. Rather than simply duplicating the structure and functions of the non-native agencies using Indian administration and staff, as other bands had done, the Spallumcheen had restored the traditional safeguards of the native community by turning for help to the band's elders and the extended families of the children who needed care and protection. "The Spallumcheen initiative has sought to re-institutionalize the functions within the extended family," the report stated.

A 1986 study funded by the Spallumcheen band showed that the child welfare program is successful. Children placed in non-native homes were returned to the band, and child welfare services are now provided within the community. The number of children needing care has been reduced. The accessibility of child welfare services has increased, but the cost of services to the band has been cut, compared to costs of provincial agencies. And, most importantly, the community has accepted the service.

## Manitoba Model

Both the federal and provincial governments have recognized the jurisdiction of the Spallumcheen band, and it is this model that Indian bands and tribal councils across the country now aspire to emulate. Despite the success of the Spallumcheen community, however, Ottawa only considers it a pilot project. The Department of Indian Affairs prefers the Manitoba example. Its tripartite master agreements — among Ottawa, the province, and tribal councils — have outlined procedures for the creation of five Indian child and family service agencies, staffed and managed by Indians, funded by Ottawa, and operating under provincial jurisdiction.

Results of the Manitoba model have been mixed. It remains the only province where more than 60,000 people, or 90 per cent of reserve residents, are served exclusively by Indian agencies. Yet some of the agencies have found themselves overwhelmed by internal and external problems and unable to duplicate the Spallumcheen success.

The agencies have discovered that sexual abuse of Indian children is a widespread problem, and they have reluctantly placed more children in foster care than they had expected. The agencies are seriously underfunded, have no programs in place to deal with sexual abuse, and are often staffed by overworked and undertrained case workers.

When the Manitoba Indian leaders negotiated the master agreements in the early 1980s, they had objectives similar to those of the Spallumcheen. They wanted to look after their own children using traditional methods, to reduce the number of placements by keeping children in extended families, and to reclaim, or repatriate as they called it, children who had been adopted into non-native homes.

There were early successes in adoptions and repatriations. Between 1983 and 1987, the number of adoptions dropped from thirty-four to seven, and almost all of these were adoptions by native families. Repatriation was a minor success, with twenty-one children being returned to their homes by 1987. The difficulty in this area arose because Manitoba refused to disclose where Indian children had been sent, claiming that its confidentiality laws prevented it from doing so. Repatriations were only possible when the adopted children told their natural parents that they wanted to return, or when natural parents were notified that their children, previously placed in foster care, were being considered for adoption.

The Manitoba agencies stumbled badly in care delivery. Nationally, the number of Indian children in care between 1976 and 1987 dropped steadily in every province except Manitoba. Since 1983, the number of Manitoba's reserve children in care has nearly doubled. The Manitoba agencies did not expect to face the complexity and severity of problems they encountered, nor were they prepared to deal with solutions. "Originally, these [child welfare] committees set out to do prevention work but really all we did was protection work — apprehend children," Ovide Mercredi explains. "We were, in essence, doing the same thing that we opposed in the first place."

One consultant's report on the work of two southern Manitoba agencies said pressure was placed on case workers to fulfil traditional expectations and still comply with provincial legislation. They failed. Between 1983 and 1987, as the five Indian agencies came into being, there was a 81 per cent increase in the number of registered Indian children in care, from 863 to 1,563. Almost 1,200 of those children had been placed by the five agencies. Meanwhile, the tripartite agreements had called for reduced budgets in the later years because Indian authorities thought the placements would dwindle. The agencies then found themselves with larger case loads and, because of the smaller budgets, fewer case workers. It was a situation ripe for tragedy.

Agency workers began to discover that children were the real victims of the social disintegration on reserves. Workers were overwhelmed with neglected and sexually abused children. Child sexual abuse referrals to the Child Protection Centre between 1981 and 1987 showed 35 per cent involved registered Indians, yet they represented only 6 per cent of the provincial population. The centre's reports concluded that the Indian solution had failed. Placing apprehended children in the homes of relatives or friends on reserves often put them in the hands of another abuser who had not yet been detected. Because the communities are so small, children were pressured by relatives and abusers to recant their stories. One report examined a six-month period in 1983-84 and found eight reserve cases that involved thirty-three victims and twenty-three offenders.

Consultant studies on four of the five new agencies during 1987 and 1988 produced similar findings. Indian case workers had little formal education. While directors and supervisors were likely to have been graduates of a recognized school of social work, most case workers — the people in the field — had not finished high school. There were federal training programs for the workers, but universities would not recognize the programs for credit because they were not offered by an accredited institution. Of the training that was offered, none was conducted in the communities where the workers lived. And because the workers had families of their own, they could not leave to take those courses. For most of them, it was on-the-job training.

"It's easy to sit on the outside and blame them and say why was the system activated before people had the basic training to do the job properly," says Dr. Sally Longstaffe, a pediatrician at Children's Hospital in Winnipeg who specializes in the treatment of abused children. "You can't blame the individual. They're doing their best. They haven't received the kind of training [they need] and they don't have the supervision and support they need."

Longstaffe says the workers wanted to help but did not know how. "We've got many, many people who are busting their rear ends but they don't know how to plan. They don't know anything about child development [in the formal sense]. They don't know how to recognize a child as being so damaged that they can't even learn. These [children] are real, living, breathing victims who can only take a certain amount [of pain] and then they're damaged permanently."

Louis Stevenson, chief of the Peguis band in Manitoba and an outspoken aboriginal leader, says that the tragedies are the inevitable part of the growing pains of the Indian community as it regains control of its own destiny. "The child-caring agencies have their growing pains too, their share of problems, but I wouldn't write any of them off because it's not any worse than what our people were subjected to previously under the Children's Aid Societies," he argues, referring to the fact that under the care and protection of Ottawa, Indian children were physically and sexually abused and tormented first in residential schools and later when the non-native child welfare agencies stepped in.

"Let an Indian have one problem and it's all blown out of proportion and the whole system is labelled [bad]," Stevenson says. "But I know better now than to let people convince me that is the case. So what if we have a few problems, it's not going to be as great as many problems that we've been subjected to ever since someone else controlled our lives."

The Manitoba bands and most of the others across the country now want independence for their agencies from provincial jurisdictions. They hope to win the freedom the Spallumcheen band has wrested from Ottawa and the British Columbia government. They have taken Ottawa's devolution policy in child welfare as far as it can go. Seeking to fulfil their self-government dreams, the Manitoba chiefs want the agencies to be accountable to their own people and hope to create a child welfare directorate, with its own culturally relevant policies and guidelines. Ottawa has rejected this model and prefers the status quo.

Stevenson, as chairman of one of the agencies, leads the Indian struggle. He encourages Indian case workers to stretch their authority off the reserves and into Winnipeg and other urban centres where their people live by licensing foster homes and approving adoptions. The case workers from the non-native agencies now find themselves fighting for Indian clients. The provincial authorities resent the intrusion and have promised court action to force the Indian agencies back on the reserve. The Indian agencies see the reserve borders as artificial boundaries and argue that the movement of their people off reserves should not prevent them from being served by their own agencies. It is a battle that can be expected to be repeated across the country as other bands try to break the ties with Ottawa and the provinces.

Though unaware of the serious problems the Manitoba Indian agencies would soon encounter, Judge Kimelman wrote in 1985 that they were better structured, in theory at least, to serve the needs of their communities than the Children's Aid Societies, which he concluded were of little value to both the non-native and native societies. Quoting from a 1984 provincial report, Kimelman said: "none of the agencies — except the Indian ones — showed sufficient sensitivity to the special cultural patterns and characteristics of the people served."

Kimelman found that the non-native agencies wrongly assumed that the norms and rules of their society should be embraced by everyone. "The cultural bias in the system for the past 40 years has made Native people victims. That must cease." The non-native agencies demanded that single native mothers live on their own if they wanted to regain custody of their children. "This demand goes against the native patterns of child care," Kimelman says, "In the Native tradition, the need of a young mother to be mothered herself is recognized. The grandparents and aunts and uncles expect the demands and rewards of raising the new member of the family. To insist that the mother remove herself from the support of her family when she needs them most is unrealistic and cruel."

Despite the damning evidence gathered in Manitoba, Indian Affairs still insists that the agencies are adequately funded. John Rayner, the department's assistant deputy minister of Indian services, said in a March 1989 interview: "I think we have a budget for the Manitoba agencies which has increased significantly over the past two or three years. And I think we feel we're funding the agencies in Manitoba to a very significant degree." Rayner claims that Ottawa wants to duplicate the Manitoba example across the country, but there is a problem with finding adequate funds to accomplish this goal.

However, eight months later, in October 1989, Indian Affairs released a report — *Indian Child and Family Services Management Regime, Discussion Paper* — outlining the direction it wants the agencies to take. The report shows Ottawa promising greater Indian autonomy but actually attempting to place the agencies under tighter control and tying them permanently to provincial jurisdiction. Like the White Paper twenty years earlier and the proposals for self-government which Ottawa unveiled in the James Bay and Sechelt agreements and Bill C-52 during the 1980s, the latest child welfare report again rejects the Indian vision of self-government. Indian leaders suspect that Ottawa is simply dismissing their demands for greater control over their own affairs.

While the 1989 child welfare report states that the government wants to create more Indian agencies, it says it does not have the funds to do so. It seeks autonomy for bands yet rejects the Spallumcheen model and demands that agencies remain under provincial jurisdiction. The paper states that funding levels will match provincial levels, but it does not take into account the need for additional staffing and training, and their associated higher costs, to ensure that Indian agencies avoid the problems documented in Manitoba.

The Indian community has taken obvious strides forward during the past ten years in establishing control of its own child welfare programs. Yet those gains were not accomplished without some errors. The consultants' reports and the professionals who have looked at the situation have concluded that what went wrong was rooted in Ottawa's unwillingness to fund serious preparation. Mistakes will always occur during a learning period, but their impact will be heightened if steps are not taken to prepare for them. The mistakes should not be held up as justification to dismantle the Indian child welfare agencies and, with them, the native dream of looking after their own children. Instead, the agencies should be seen as the only way that Indian people will come to grips with their problems. More funds, more training, and more time are needed.

# 9

# Justice

Alvert Cherry slouches in his chair and listens intently to the man sitting next to him who is translating into English the lyrical Ojibway Cherry has just uttered. The translation holds the attention of the 100 witnesses almost as easily as Cherry's own hypnotic tones did. When it is finished, Cherry leans forward to make another point, his face falling into silhouette in front of the large, barred window behind him.

It is April 12, 1989, and Cherry, an inmate of Stony Mountain Federal Penitentiary in Manitoba, has about fifteen minutes to have his say before the Aboriginal Justice Inquiry which is investigating native experiences in the province's justice system. But Cherry's time stretches far beyond that. The inquiry's commissioners, associate chief provincial court judge Murray Sinclair, an Ojibway Indian with a long braid stretching down his back, and Justice Alvin Hamilton of the Manitoba Court of the Queen's Bench, a silver-haired white man, appear to be in no rush as they take down copious notes.

Amid the day's stories of mistreatment and discrimination, and various opinions on how to improve a justice system that incarcerates Canada's aboriginal people at phenomenal rates, one theme begins to emerge beyond all others. And it is Cherry, speaking quietly and simply with the authority of a philosopher king, who brings together the unconnected statements of the native inmates who live behind the sandblasted walls of this century-old institution and of the hundreds of others who have appeared before the commission in the months before. "The white man has been here for 500 years," Cherry says. "It is about time that the white man starts to learn about our different culture."

Throughout the day, the judges have heard about many instances of the prison system's lack of understanding and acceptance of native traditions and beliefs: spiritual ceremonies that are restricted to once a week, following the Christian custom of worshipping only on Sunday; the removal of sweet grass and medicine bags in cell searches; having only one elder available to satisfy a diversity of native traditions (including the sweat lodge ceremony, which can only be held once a month because one man cannot handle this physically taxing ceremony more often).

With these examples and several of his own, Cherry illustrates just how foreign the white society's concept of incarceration is to the native inmate and how prison not only removes him from society, but meters out additional punishment by placing him in a system that fails to reflect the values of native people. "We have our own values, our own way of life as aboriginal people," Cherry concludes in accented English. "We are in a very abnormal setting."

Weeks later, as the public hearings segment of the Manitoba inquiry winds up, Judge Sinclair reflects on the 800 presentations. "We have been told that we must look seriously at the ways that our justice system has come to grips with what has often been a matter of cultures in conflict," says Sinclair.

An acceptance that there might be something inherently unjust, discriminatory, and racist in forcing non-native rules of incarceration and methods of rehabilitation on native people stands as the most profound notion to have emerged from more than two decades of studies of native involvement in Canada's complex legal system, including interactions with police, the courts, prisons, parole boards, and social service agencies. A look at the studies of the past twenty years shows a plethora of examinations into every conceivable native justice issue, viewed from every angle, with a mountain of suggestions, often very similar, about how to change things. However, as with most native issues, actual change has been agonizingly slow to materialize, and native Canadians look at the growing mountain of documentation simply as further evidence to support their often repeated lament: "We have been studied to death with little to show for it."

It was in the late 1960s, in the glow of the civil rights movement in the United States, that Canada began to take a look at its own civil rights record. Was racism behind the disproportionate number of incarcerated native people?? Or was it simply poverty that was the root cause?? In search of answers and ways to dissipate the building tensions among native people, federal and provincial governments in Canada began conducting internal reviews on everything from hiring practices at all levels of the justice system to the treatment of native offenders at the hands of the RCMP, local police, and all levels of the judiciary.

In 1975, the first (and to date only) attempt to explore the issue on a national scale took place during a three-day federal-provincial conference in Edmonton, Alberta. The National Conference on Native Peoples and the Criminal Justice System attracted more than 200 delegates, including former solicitor general of Canada Warren Allmand, his provincial counterparts, and native leaders from across Canada. "Our expectations of this conference are high, and so they should be," Allmand stated. "We share a determination to gain a better understanding of the problems we face and to move towards their solution."

The conference's six general guidelines and fifty-eight specific recommendations covered everything from the need to hire more native people throughout the criminal justice system to teaching non-native people already working in the system about aboriginal customs and values. These suggestions reflected, in somewhat more detail, many of the same concerns and possible solutions raised two years earlier in the Conference on Northern Justice conducted in Manitoba.

Throughout the 1980s, the number and intensity of the examinations accelerated. In 1988, the solicitor general's department was nearing the end of a two-year study into the experience of native offenders from the day they entered federal prison to their release. The interim report, based on interviews with inmates and staff at all levels, again issued the call for more native staff and involvement in programs and the need to educate non-native staff to encourage respect for aboriginal people.

## Public Attention Focused

Despite the repetition of studies and apparent lack of progress, many experts agree that the accumulation of this mountain of evidence has finally focused public attention on native justice issues. For example, in the late 1980s Canadians were being bombarded almost daily by the extensive publicity surrounding three independent province-wide examinations of the treatment of native offenders at the hands of the judiciary.

In Manitoba, the government launched the Aboriginal Justice Inquiry after the March 1988 shooting death of native leader John Joseph Harper by a Winnipeg constable. For months on end, Canadians watched as almost every level of the justice system, from the courts to police, were scrutinized as never before.

In Nova Scotia, a two-year, $7-million study of the circumstances surrounding the wrongful conviction of Donald Marshall, Jr., a Nova Scotia Micmac Indian who served eleven years in prison for a murder he did not commit, released a scathing report that touched every level of Nova Scotia's judicial system. "The criminal justice system failed Donald Marshall Jr. at virtually every turn," concluded the three Nova Scotia judges in their seven-volume report released on January 26, 1990. And they said, in no uncertain terms, that racism had played a major role in Marshall's conviction and incarceration.

And in April 1988, the Alberta government buckled after ten months of pressure and called for an inquiry into police relations with the province's aboriginal people. One of its specific mandates was to examine a claim by the Blood Indians that police had improperly conducted murder investigations involving band members. Less than three weeks before the inquiry was to get underway, an additional spark was added to the already tense situation when a Lethbridge policeman shot and killed a Blood Indian named Heavy Runner, after the man threatened police with a pair of knives. What was to have been a six-month probe into five mysterious deaths ended eleven months later with more than 15,000 pages of transcripts and 160 exhibits on sixteen deaths. As with so many other examinations into native issues in Canada, the $2-million inquiry, led by Provincial Court Judge Carl Rolph, grew to explore the wide-ranging problems facing the Blood Indian band, from alcohol abuse to poverty.

And the pressure showed no signs of abating, as several other Indian leaders across Canada called for similar inquiries in their own jurisdictions. Legal experts predict the conclusions and recommendations stemming from such inquiries will have wide-ranging implications for the entire country. Professor Michael Jackson of the University of British Columbia says he is confident that each of the reviews will have a greater impact than simply one of releasing tensions and allowing things to settle back down again. "We are on the verge of a breakthrough," he argues. "There is just too much going on around the country. The 1975 conference was not much more than people coming together. There was no sustained effort."

Although the examinations add new twists based on individual circumstances, all have moved beyond the specific workings of the machinery of justice and into the complex connections between poverty, discrimination, crime, and imprisonment. No new or startling revelations about why so many native people are imprisoned are expected, nor are any miracle cures. But, according to legal and other experts, what is new is an emerging collective notion among Canadians and legal minds that it may be time to give native people a turn in handling a problem whites have had little success with. Attached to this admission is another more striking one — that native customs, methods, and values have credibility and are more likely to be more effective tools of rehabilitation for the large numbers of native people housed in the country's prisons and correctional institutions than the traditional non-native approach.

The law offers a distinct view of how native notions of self-government would eventually fit into the wider Canadian context. Indian leaders seeking some control over native justice always speak of models and programs that follow the basic laws of the land — the Criminal Code as well as provincial laws and regulations. There is not, for example, a native movement to make Indian reserves into separate political and legal entities where armed robbery or rape would not be considered crimes. The models being examined and discussed by native leaders and academics involve working within the Canadian legal system, which is similar to the way the independent U.S. tribal courts and reserve-based courts work as arms of the federal government. In the U.S., the courts are structured by the various communities to reflect their own traditions. They use their own legal codes and frequently rely on traditional customs to reach decisions. Some even have their own jails. However, the maximum penalties tribal courts can impose are one-year jail terms or $500 fines. Serious crimes such as murder and assault are dealt with by the federal courts.

A major signal that these ideas have put down some serious roots in Canada was the 1988 report by the staunchly conservative Canadian Bar Association, *Locking Up Natives in Canada*, which after a two-year study endorsed the idea that native people should be given the opportunity to run their own court systems. Similar admissions in other areas, grudging as they may have been over the past twenty years, have resulted in slow, but definite changes in the degree of Indian control over education, child welfare, and self-government. Only the area of health care lags further behind justice and law in dealing with the issue of native control.

Professor Michael Jackson, author of the Canadian Bar Association report, claims that the law is probably the most rigidly conservative institution in the western world and, like health care, is one of the more intimidating institutions to consider taking over for any group. "Sometimes these communities have the least ability to do something about it because they have so many other responsibilities, so many other issues to deal with that the idea of taking over the justice system is overwhelming. Justice takes a back seat, it seems intractable. It is fairly daunting to take on when you have no jobs, when your kids are dropping out of school, your people are on welfare."

Still, even if native people aren't yet ready to take on the full responsibilities of a justice system, work must begin. "What we tried to do in the Canadian Bar report was not to question native priorities, and not to suggest that if they all had tribal courts all the other problems would go away," Jackson emphasizes. "But I think that while these other initiatives play out, there are other things that can be done in justice to buttress those other initiatives."

As Jackson claims, the idea of altering the justice system by offering culturally appropriate programs suggests a shift in power. And power is something that is never relinquished easily. "It is the most cohesive part of a state's apparatus, the exercise of punitive power," says one law professor. "It is always difficult to wrest power from the people who have it. The criminal justice system is awfully resistant to change."

According to Judge Murray Sinclair, who co-chaired Manitoba's Aboriginal Justice Inquiry, moving into a position where the dominant society hands over the power has less to do with native people demonstrating an ability to handle the task (as many bureaucrats suggest) and more to do with a change in thinking on the part of the dominant society. "I think the real question is whether the people who had control of the football are prepared to hand it off. We have to understand that the process of self-government is one they [native people] are inherently familiar with. It has been part of their life for generations. What has not been part of the system is the respect for their history." This respect for native ways is what must evolve before real change can take place, Sinclair argues. "Not merely respect for it in the sense of it's all nice and thank you very much for telling me, but a trust in it and a faith in it and a willingness to divest and give up control where control now rests."

The specific issue of native incarceration was not in the forefront of discussion when the 1969 White Paper was

released. The document itself makes no mention of the issue
of the incarceration of native people, and the subject does not
appear in the thousands of pages of White Paper briefs, memos,
letters, and planned strategies which circled around Ottawa at
the time. However, in its 196-page response to the
government's proposals, *Wahbung, Our Tomorrow*, which was
presented to the federal government more than a year later, the
Manitoba Indian Brotherhood offered a few thoughts on the
subject.

Referring to a study of native offences and the number of
native inmates in the province, the document noted that, in
1969, Indians made up about 4 per cent of Manitoba's population and just over 1 per cent in the Winnipeg area, but they
accounted for 23 per cent of the 5,472 people involved in a
variety of offences in the city and 19 per cent of the 4,302 held
in Headingley Jail, half of whom were being held for failing to
pay fines. Two decades later, the statistics were even worse. At
Headingley in 1987, status Indians accounted for 25 per cent
of the 2,703 prisoners. Including Métis in the count,
Headingley's population, which houses prisoners serving sentences of two years less a day, was more than 41 per cent
aboriginal. Research continued to undercover large numbers
who had been jailed for failing to pay fines.

In 1988, Statistics Canada reported that native offenders
accounted for at least 11 per cent of all admissions to federal
penitentiaries while making up less than 3 per cent of the
national population. Officials in the corrections department say
that, for a variety of reasons, many inmates refuse to admit to
their native heritage and that the rate is in fact higher. When
Alvert Cherry appeared before Manitoba's justice inquiry, a
corrections official estimated that more than 40 per cent of
Stony Mountain inmates were of aboriginal origin, including
status, non-status, Métis, and Inuit, based on information
provided voluntarily by the inmates. Aboriginal people made
up just under 10 per cent of Manitoba's 1.07 million population
according to the 1986 census.

## Pattern of Incarceration

The pattern of incarceration reflects the distribution of native people across the country. East of the prairie provinces, no more than 5 per cent of inmates in any one province were native in 1987-88, while native people accounted for between 12 and 36 per cent of admissions in Manitoba, Alberta, and British Columbia and for over 50 per cent in Saskatchewan, Yukon, and the Northwest Territories. The rate of incarceration in provincial jails, where inmates serve sentences of less than two years, is even more striking. In 1987-88 aboriginal people made up 18 per cent of provincial inmate populations across the country. Again the numbers follow the east-west pattern: less than 10 per cent of inmates in the eastern provinces were aboriginal compared to over 50 per cent in Manitoba, Saskatchewan, the Yukon, and N.W.T.

According to Michael Jackson, some people argue that dealing with these disproportionate figures by having a separate native justice system would amount to an unequal or privileged treatment of one group, in contravention of Sect. 15 (1) of the Charter of Rights and Freedoms. But these people, he says, have missed the point. "The numbers alone tell us that quite distinctly what we have is a denial of equality." What is missing in the other view, Jackson argues, is an understanding that native people have distinctive rights and status as the first citizens of this country, rights that were recognized in another section of the Constitution, rights that are not shared by ethnic groups in the country. "There is a constitutional basis for it for native people and there is not a constitutional basis for other groups." Here Jackson is referring to Sect. 35 of the Constitution and its recognition of basic aboriginal rights.

The lack of understanding of this key element in the whole argument reaches the highest levels of both the judiciary and government, and it is one of the major stumbling blocks to progress, Jackson argues. In January 1989, as Canada's newly appointed Conservative Minister of Justice, Doug Lewis revealed that he had failed to grasp this central notion: he claimed that a parallel justice system for natives could unleash a series of similar requests from other groups.

Michael Jackson also believes that the native people's struggle to control their own justice system is hampered by the large number of native offenders. Based on their interactions with native offenders, the people involved at all levels of the judiciary, the same people who will ultimately have to agree to relinquish power, have the distinct notion that Indian people cannot possibly handle such a complex affair as the administration of justice. "Those in criminal justice typically see native people at the worst part of their lives," Jackson says. "Police, sheriffs, judges, and prison staff don't see native communities and their leadership solving their own problems. They see the people who have failed. They rarely come into contact with the native leaders responding to problems in positive, effective ways. From that viewpoint, the response is predictable: 'How can native people do this when they can't stand up straight?'"

Besides this kind of misunderstanding, there are the questions about the nuts and bolts of a native-run justice system: what would it look like and how would it operate? The traditional native justice system is rooted in the aboriginal emphasis on co-operation, unlike the adversarial basis of the white justice system. Such co-operation was key to the survival of small Indian tribes leading a nomadic life in the days before the Europeans arrived. While the traditional native justice system handed out punishment, it also worked to maintain the cohesiveness and survival of the smaller group. Imprisonment was and (continues to be) viewed as a destructive measure that harms not only the accused, but also the community. Historically, various forms of ridicule before the larger group were used, everything from forcing a public apology to banishment from the group for a period of time. Customary punishments handed out in the U.S. system include direct or indirect restitution to the victim of the crime or community work.

When Jackson's 119-page report for the Canadian Bar Association was released, the media immediately latched on to one suggestion: a return to a separate, totally native-run justice system. But that was only one model among several presented in the document. And it was never Jackson's intention to suggest that Canada's aboriginal people have to agree to one system. Demanding that native people accept only one model disregards the vast diversity of aboriginal bands across the country. Canada's aboriginal people have many common roots, but they speak different languages, have different customs, a multitude of traditions and histories, and various needs.

While the media focused on the most extreme native justice model to highlight the issues, the federal government ignored the expert comments on aboriginal diversity and consistently maintained that Indians present a unified position. "The government keeps asking why they can't agree about what they want," Michael Jackson says. "There is this idea that somehow there should be this one model. Well, it is something they can't come up with."

## Still More Problems

There is yet another problem adding to the slow progress in designing a native-based justice system. According to Jennifer Brown, a University of Winnipeg anthropologist specializing in native history, creating a new justice system based totally on native traditions is probably not possible. For one thing, some native traditions have been lost forever, and even if they could be rediscovered, approaches that worked in the past would often not work in today's context. "I really think what you've got more of is a kind of innovation and adaptation," she says. "If people attempted to reconstruct tribal justice, it could be a form of justice that would incorporate quite a few traditional values and concerns and themes of native culture, but the actual form would have to mesh with what life is like now. One could go back to the traditionalist-oriented kind of system that would preserve certain themes, but I don't think it would be appropriate to call it traditional."

Brown sees evidence that the native community is well aware of these problems and is working towards a system that would operate in co-operation with the Canadian justice system. "I think the native people are part of a world-wide phenomenon. They have suffered the impact of other groups coming in, sometimes in a very heavy-handed way, and ways have to be found to adapt to that, on both sides," she says. "History is not a reel of film you can run backwards."

Michael Jackson agrees. Old methods of punishment such as public ridicule worked in a world where offenders cared deeply about what their peers thought. "How do you bring community pressure to bear when someone is not amenable to it? It requires new solutions." Jackson also claims that native groups are not seeking answers that will isolate them from the rest of the country, but are looking for opportunities to develop justice systems in co-operation with the larger society.

The Canadian government doesn't have to look far to find examples of different models or for evidence that various models can thrive within a larger framework. As part of their research, Judge Sinclair and Justice Hamilton took their inquiry south of the border to study the tribal court system run by the Navaho and Pueblo Indians.

Sinclair notes that U.S. bands have been able to support their own justice systems despite the fact that the majority have a population of only 500 people. About half of Canada's band populations are over 500, with several in the 1,000 to 5,000 range. "Many of them have their own tribal courts," Sinclair says of the U.S. system. "But they don't have full-time court administrators, they don't have full-time probation workers, they don't have full-time parole officers, they don't have a full-time jail, they don't have a full-time sheriff. What they do is rent. They rent a justice system. They generally rent a justice system from another tribe, an adjacent tribe with a similar culture."

Judge Sinclair and Justice Hamilton visited several Pueblo Communities in Arizona and New Mexico. The largest had a population of about 3,200 and its own full-time judge. "But the other Pueblos don't. They don't have the resources or the money or the crime to afford all of their own systems," Judge Sinclair notes. Instead, the smaller Pueblo communities rent time from the full-time judge, who uses the money to hire a part-time judge when necessary. Also rented as part of the contract are a prosecutor and a legal aid officer.

The difference between the U.S. system and the circuit court system in Canada is that all the judicial players are Pueblos who spend up to a week in the communities they serve and they are paid by the bands. In Canada, few native people are among the provincially sponsored court parties that fly into isolated reserves in the morning and out again at night. "The result is that these people don't feel like part of the community, don't feel answerable to the community. They don't feel any connection to the clients," says Sinclair, repeating one of the most common complaints about the circuit system.

Michael Jackson's report notes that the U.S. has three Indian court systems — traditional courts, Courts of Indian Offences, and tribal courts — each of which offers insights into the potential problems of any proposed Canadian native justice system. There are eighteen traditional or customary courts operating among the Pueblos of the American southwest. The tribal governor of the Pueblos acts as a judge, enforcing laws based on longstanding traditions. The Pueblos have no written constitution or codes of offences, and customary law is handed down through oral tradition. The governor is appointed annually by the Pueblo council, a body composed of ex-governors.

The Courts of Indian Offences were first established by the U.S. government in 1883. They were part of an effort to destroy aboriginal culture by outlawing plural marriages, weakening the influence of medicine men, "civilizing" the Indians, and teaching them respect for private property by breaking up communal or tribal landholdings. The aim was to have a court for every tribal government, a goal that was almost reached (seventeen still exist). Courts were staffed by Indian Agents who applied the law according to a criminal and civil code drafted by the Indian Commissioner. Customary Indian law was ignored or outlawed.

Today, Indians are fighting to wrestle back control. The U.S. Bureau of Indian Affairs appoints all judges to four-year terms, but the appointments are subject to the approval of the tribal council. All relevant federal laws, rulings of the Department of the Interior, and any tribal regulations or customs that don't conflict with federal laws are applied as are provisions of the

Code of Indian Tribal Offences established by the federal government.

The system has faced a number of criticisms. One is that, because few written decisions are executed, case law has failed to develop any precedents. And issues of conflict of interest, a question that has been raised in the Canadian debate, have surfaced with charges that political or family considerations have interfered with the court's decisions.

An about-face in U.S. government thinking in the 1930s led to the Indian Reorganization Act of 1934. This movement to return some autonomy to Indians resulted in establishment of the tribal court system. The act allowed, among other things, for each tribe to enact laws governing internal matters, and this led many to adopt their own tribal court system. However, it was assumed that any laws would be based on western and not on aboriginal customs and concepts. To this end, the Bureau of Indian Affairs drafted criminal code models, and with limited resources to evaluate the codes, tribes simply adopted them. In recent years, however, many tribes have redesigned their laws to align them more closely with their self-determination goals.

Michael Jackson's report explores village courts in Papua, New Guinea, some overseas examples, the Australian aboriginal court system, and limited Canadian experiences — notably the Akwesasne (formerly St. Regis) and Kahnawake bands in Quebec. The Australian model basically adapted the country's court structure by creating special courts for aborigines. These courts, however, did not reflect existing aboriginal authority structures, but simply adapted the regular court system to account for what was deemed the special situation of aborigines. Jackson notes that the motivation behind the creation of the special courts was suspect. The Australian Law Reform Commission suggested that one reason for creating the courts was because judges in ordinary courts were reluctant to convict the poverty-stricken aborigines and more convictions would result in the special courts.

In Canada, two Quebec Mohawk bands have been running their own justice system for several years by applying Criminal

Code and band bylaw violations under section 107 of the Indian Act, a section originally designed to aid government assimilation plans. Fines levied are paid to the band government, and prison terms are dealt with through an arrangement with the Quebec government. But Jackson argues that section 107, which established in 1881 that all Indian agents and their superiors within Indian Affairs were automatically appointed justices of the peace under the Indian Act with powers to impose rules and regulations under the act, was triggered by a motivation similar to that which sparked the U.S. move to establish Courts of Indian Offences as a means of "civilizing the Indian population." Section 107 is, therefore, unacceptable as a basis for launching a native-made model.

Jackson also finds serious problems with attempting, as some bands have done, to test their legal jurisdiction under sections 81 and 83 of the Indian Act which allow the bands to set bylaws. Although bands have won a measure of success by using the bylaws to challenge federal fishing regulations and some provincial laws, Jackson notes that the bylaws affect only registered Indians within the jurisdictions of reserves and that under the Indian Act the Minister of Indian Affairs has the power to disallow any bylaws. Although Jackson's report presents some models that would work within this and other existing legislative frameworks, he argues that, ultimately, the government must introduce new legislation to make a native justice system workable. This would, of course, require a degree of co-operation and understanding on the part of the federal and provincial governments that has not yet been seen in the native justice debate.

Meanwhile, the inquiries drag on, and the studies, the recommendations, and the frustrations continue to pile up. The Marshall inquiry, in particular, has stripped away any notions that Marshall's experience was an isolated incident. The underlying problems of racism have been exposed for all to see.

Judge Sinclair sits in his Winnipeg office, speaking slowly, calmly, and with great patience about "how, as an aboriginal person, I feel this anger, and frustration and sense of wanting to strike out." Instead of lashing out, however, he finds himself guiding other native people in directing those kinds of feelings as a way of changing things. "What we have said to [native] people in the course of our inquiry is that our report stays on the shelf as long as you're prepared to allow it to stay there. We expect that the inherent tendency of government will be to file it away and forget about it."

Judge Sinclair maintains that the inquiry is a small contribution to the overall process of change, and part of it is simply to get Canadians thinking about aboriginal people, and getting native people talking among themselves. "I may go to my death bed never knowing if I accomplished those things. But I think I've contributed towards their accomplishment."

What about a sense of urgency, of frustration after so many inquiries and studies and lack of action? "You have to understand the native culture. Urgency is not a concept.... I don't know of any tribe that has a word for it. Patience is the virtue. The time in which things get done is less relevant than the doing. The point is that inherently there's a faith in our culture, in the outcome of life."

And, perhaps more relevant this time around, is something Sinclair said in his closing remarks at the end of the first part of the year-long inquiry. "We believe that, now, everybody is listening."

# 10

# Native Organizations

Political organizations are the machines of real action in a democratic society. They target issues, orchestrate lobby efforts and force change in a complex world. In the past two decades, native leaders and their organizations have emerged from near obscurity to become the active and increasingly effective voices of Canada's native people.

There were about fourteen fledgling native political organizations across the country when the White Paper made its debut in Ottawa in 1969, including two national organizations — the National Indian Brotherhood and the Canadian Métis Society. Together they made up the National Indian Council which had been formed in 1954. In 1968, the two groups went their separate ways: the National Indian Brotherhood moved on to foster the growth of the identity and culture of status Indians; the Canadian Métis Society began lobby efforts on behalf of all other aboriginal people. In the early days, native organizations survived on a lot of passion and the little money they could scrape together. Their leaders may have been household names in their own communities, but they were little known elsewhere. Their political battles were usually one-on-one affairs with Ottawa bureaucrats — or with each other. By 1989, the number of native political bodies had grown to at least twenty-one, plus the Assembly of First Nations, the renamed and reorganized National Indian Brotherhood.

From their crises-oriented beginnings, native organizations have evolved into sophisticated lobby groups capable of launching and winning intricate court battles over everything from constitutional amendments to land claims and fishing rights. They have become masters at public relations. Some things, however, have not changed. There is still the same passion that fed the organizations throughout the 1960s. Their funding struggles now involve much larger sums but are nevertheless similar to those that hampered their efforts from the very beginning. They continue to be the target of government manipulation. And, despite twenty years of practice, the organizations still suffer some discomfort working within the complex, cumbersome white bureaucracy.

During the past twenty years, three political events have helped shape the evolution of native organizations: the 1969 White Paper; the repatriation of the Canadian Constitution; and the Meech Lake Accord, a document native leaders viewed as a threat.

Native organizations were one of the few specific targets in the White Paper. Federal bureaucrats made it clear that they expected these groups, as young and inexperienced as some of them were, to act as the main conduits for implementing the government's complex plan. Native organizations, particularly those with a specifically political mandate, had been offered little encouragement from Ottawa before the White Paper policy was announced, especially when it came to funding. That all changed in 1969: Ottawa had a new policy to sell, and bureaucrats and politicians decided they needed strong provincial and national native groups to get the job done. "The Government proposed to invite the executives of the National Indian Brotherhood and the various provincial associations to discuss the role they might play in the implementation of the new policy, and the financial resources they may require," states the final page of the White Paper.

Money began to flow. Ottawa offered the financially strapped Indian groups a grant package of $1 per capita for provincial organizations and 25 cents per capita for the National Indian Brotherhood. A total of $300,000 was made available

to the associations in the first year of what was to be a multi-
year program and included additional funding for special meetings held to discuss the White Paper proposals. Eventually, the
government planned to provide funds directly to bands, which
would in turn pass money on to the groups they supported.
There appeared to be no thought given to the bickering this
kind of financial setup could, and would, lead to among the
poverty-stricken groups.

Indian organizations with a purely political mandate began
to multiply after the White Paper. Those heading the organizations stopped being mere advisers to Ottawa; they became
leaders representing native demands. The groups were descen-
dants of early organizations which rose and fell, regrouped, and
rose again from the time of the earliest recorded native political
body — the Allied Indian Tribes of British Columbia —
formed in 1915, to the 1981 formation of the Assembly of First
Nations, an association of chiefs across the country. Its precur-
sor, the National Indian Brotherhood, had been an association
of bands, a role that was taken over during the 1970s by provincially based tribal councils and other regional associations.

Optimists viewed the 1969 financing arrangement, like most
of the White Paper, as a gross display of naiveté on the part of
the federal bureaucracy and its energetic new minister. Scep-
tics, on the other hand, believed the plan revealed the
government's hidden agenda of forcing assimilation on
Canada's native people: the native political machinery was
being funded so it could carry out the assimilation plan which,
if successful, would make the organizations obsolete. Either
way, the plan contained several miscalculations.

First was the federal government's absolute confidence that,
with a little encouragement, native organizations would come
to support the changes proposed by the White Paper. To native
leaders, this miscalculation was yet another example of the
government's failure to hear what Indian people had been
saying for decades about self-determination. There was also
Chrétien's assumption that, by 1969, the Indian political infrastructure had evolved to the point where it could function
like a government bureaucracy. Under Chrétien's plan, the

money-starved Indian bands would be given funds to support organizations which in turn would lobby on their behalf at the government's bargaining table.

In 1969, that financing strategy translated into $61,000 base funding for the National Indian Brotherhood. In 1989, after an often bumpy financial ride which included some serious debts, the Assembly of First Nations survived on an annual balanced budget of over $3.5 million from a variety of sources. More than half a million came directly from Ottawa in the same style of support as the 1969 funds. In 1990 this budget became the target of federal cost-cutting measures.

The funding of provincial groups followed a similar twenty-year course. In 1969, the newly created Union of British Columbia Indians was the recipient of $46,046. By the late 1970s, the union had become something of a bureaucratic monster, with about eighty staff and a $1.2 million budget. A few years later, the union was hit with serious financial problems, many of them linked to its lobbying efforts in the 1982 battle to repatriate the Constitution and to the recession of the early 1980s. In 1989, the monster had been tamed, says its leader. Seven full-time employees and six contract staff were surviving on about $600,000 a year.

Federal funding for Indian political organizations has always been a hotly debated issue. Native leaders have had to face the contradiction of accepting funding from the people or body that their groups lobby against. Native leaders in the late 1960s were aware of the potential trap they were entering when Ottawa first held out its hand. But with few resources and a membership heavily dependent on federal assistance programs, the leaders decided they had little choice but to accept the financial help of the federal government in order to build their own political infrastructures. The authors of the White Paper were evidently aware of the scepticism of native leaders and included in their plan a long-term goal in which native organizations would be funded by their own bands and eventually by the grassroots itself. This grassroots financial support would remove native organizations from direct support from the government.

In 1969, Indian Affairs Minister Jean Chrétien believed that the White Paper plan would lift the majority of native people out of poverty within thirty years. Although the White Paper gave no specific time-frame, Ottawa seemed to believe that Indians would be able to afford to support their own lobby groups within this same thirty-year period. "In this way we ensure that all the Indian organizations are independent," Chrétien said of future funding plans. "We want money to come from the grassroots, and eventually it must, but many Indian people cannot yet afford to support the associations so we will feed the money in at the band level and let them decide who will speak for them, and what they want to have said."

And all might have gone according to plan if the young and mostly inexperienced native groups had not been so successful in their fight against the White Paper. For what many researchers and historians believe was the first time, Indians across the country put aside their differing interests and united as one voice. Their written response to the Chrétien document took them almost a year to develop. They wrote hundreds of letters, lobbied the Queen, called on international bodies to hear their charges, and, on occasion, they threatened federal bureaucrats with violence. And it worked. Ottawa shelved Chrétien's White Paper and launched a search for new ground one year after the paper was released and soon after native leaders handed over to the goverment three major studies on the directions the government should take. The search is still on. And in the political vacuum that has existed on native issues since 1970, native groups have slowly transformed themselves into fierce challengers who are never far from centre stage.

In his book *Native People in Canada: Contemporary Conflicts*, James Frideres traces the roots of modern native political bodies back to the nineteenth century and the efforts of native people to form regional and national organizations capable of representing their interests at various forums. According to Frideres, there were two basic reasons for the eventual demise of the early groups — federal suppression and internal disharmony within native organizations.

The disharmony within native organizations, noted Frideres and other historians, is linked to the numerous divisions that naturally exist within such diverse groups as Canada's original people. Their histories and experiences across the land have been different. They speak twelve different languages and their religious beliefs, while often similar, are not identical. They come from numerous tribes and a variety of regions, both rural and urban. On top of this, they have been forced to live according to white labels attached to them — from Métis to non-treaty, treaty, status, and non-status. Despite all of these differences, however, native people have become increasingly aware of the power of presenting a united front to white society.

## Attempts Thwarted

Attempts to unite over the centuries have been thwarted by more than just the enormity of the task of bringing together such a diverse population. Evidence of manipulation — both official and non-official — by federal officials to prevent the emergence of a political native force has been well-documented. One of the most blatant moves was the Indian Act of 1927 which prohibited native people from organizing politically beyond the local level. But even today, forty years after the restriction was removed, there is ample evidence that Ottawa continues to manipulate the progress of native political organizations according to its own agenda. Funding for well-established groups can be cut off with little notice while new groups who are friendlier to Ottawa suddenly find cash in their accounts. Federal bureaucrats have also been known to support or instigate smear campaigns against native leaders who have caused them grief.

These competing tensions between native groups and the federal government were well-entrenched by the time Ottawa released the White Paper. The policy paper offered a clear example of how bureaucrats hoped to support the groups and how they worried that the divisions within the neophyte organizations would make their plan more difficult to carry out. Wrote one Indian Affairs supervisor to his federal masters a month after the White Paper's release: "A surprising result of the Policy Statement has been the discrediting of the New Brunswick Association in the eyes of many Indians. It was reported that some Indians blame the association for the policy and have already resigned from it. The association is fairly new.... If it falls by the wayside, we will be confronted with extra difficulties in embarking on the consultation and negotiation process in that province." No mention was made of how the loss of the association would affect the ability of New Brunswick natives to voice their concerns.

Harold Cardinal, who was the dynamic, determined, twenty-four-year-old leader of the Indian Association of Alberta in 1969, believes that Canadians often forget just how new native people are to the white political game. It was not until 1951 that the government removed from the Indian Act some of the restrictions preventing native political development: the right of Indians to organize outside of their reserves, their right to leave reserves without getting permission from their Indian agent, and the right of others to help Indians prepare claims against the government without legal penalty. "Those were part of a total range of instruments that the Canadian government was using as a policy to wipe out Indianness," Cardinal argued in 1989, referring to federal policies throughout the 1930s and 1940s. "In 1951, it was clear that those kinds of laws could not be tolerated anymore. And, in a sense, that began the long, slow climb back."

The other major break, according to Cardinal, came in 1960 when Indians were given, for the first time, the right to vote in federal elections. Native people had already gained provincial and territorial voting rights in British Columbia, Nova Scotia, Newfoundland, the Northwest Territories (1949), and in Ontario (1954). Those rights would come later in the Yukon, Manitoba, and Saskatchewan (1960), in New Brunswick and Prince Edward Island (1963), in Alberta (1965), and in Quebec (1969). But it was the 1960 federal benchmark that Cardinal and other native leaders view as the key that finally unlocked the door to true growth for native political organizations in the modern Canadian context: "With the granting of the franchise, that signalled the nation state's acceptance that we might be human after all," says Cardinal sardonically.

The native vote came amid the early signs that times were changing across North America. The black rights movement in the United States, a revolution underscored by the introduction of the 1964 Civil Rights Act, was having an impact on the Indian rights movement in Canada. "I don't think our elders ever lost their sense of who they were individually, or collectively," says Cardinal, recalling his own political awakening during that era. "But the 1960s made it possible for them to very cautiously come out into the open from their catacombs recognizing that there may be a chance of living and practising the kinds of things they have been striving to protect through those years."

Cardinal is one of several native leaders and other observers who bristle at the suggestion that it was the White Paper that turned Indian organizations into effective lobby groups and also at the suggestion that the Ottawa policy had anything to do with the evolution of Indian leadership. Cardinal points out that, before the White Paper was drawn up, the first national Indian body — the National Indian Brotherhood — was already emerging as an organization prepared to fight for Indian rights and the protection of Indian culture. All the policy did, he says, was force native leaders to regroup and focus their energies on fighting the latest government threat instead of on the goals they had set for themselves. Others, however, credit the government announcement for their very existence.

Indian organizations in British Columbia have had a troubled past, with groups frequently divided on religious or other lines or torn by fights over limited funding and attention. Still, the Union of British Columbia Indians celebrated its twentieth anniversary in August 1989. The union is one group that links its origins to the White Paper policy. Saul Terry, union president and chief of the Pine River Band, described the birth of the union in 1969: "The idea was to pull all people together because of the fact the government was taking an action we did not think was conducive to our continued existence. I guess there was a common focus around which people were able to rally. It pulled people together for a time and broke down the traditional barriers."

Some historians say that the birth of modern native political organizations is more likely the result of a number of factors, from the civil rights movement to the much-hated residential school system, which took native children from their homes and force-fed them a non-native philosophy and language. "I don't think you can go to one cause," says Jennifer Brown, anthropologist and history professor at the University of Winnipeg. "There is an interesting generational factor," Brown explains, adding that, in a perverse sort of way, the much-maligned residential schools could be partly credited with helping native people from a variety of backgrounds reach some sense of consensus about their goals, problems, and potential solutions. "A lot of young people were brought together from different reserves. They had common problems and they all underwent this sort of shared initiation. They began to share views."

In Manitoba, David Courchene, Sr., along with Harold Cardinal in Alberta and Walter Dieter in Saskatchewan, spearheaded the battle against the White Paper in the provincial groups as well as in the newly formed National Indian Brotherhood. Courchene remembers the early days of organizing the national body the year before the White Paper policy was released and loves to reminisce about the heady days of travelling from community to community, full of the desire to change the desperate conditions of Indian life. Although Ojibwa, Chippeway, Cree, and Sioux were spoken in most of the Manitoba communities he visited, Courchene says the meetings he held across the province were largely conducted in halting English. "There was no money and no budget," says Courchene, who was the chief of the Fort Alexander reserve by the time the national organization was officially established in late 1967. "We used to have to pass the hat around in the community to get to the next community. But I was never short of a bed, or food, or smoke. It took me a year to get organized." According to Courchene, Indians across the country were being guided towards the national goal by the head of the twenty-year-old

Saskatchewan Indian Association, Walter Dieter, who would serve as the first National Indian Brotherhood president. "We were into an exciting political, social, and philosophical state of development," says Cardinal, the youngest of the dynamic trio. "We went out with a sense of adventure."

The three were the first of a new breed of native leader. Educated in the white school system and wise to the workings of the federal bureaucracy, they struck a common chord among their people. Courchene recalls that native people were hungry to organize. "Getting together was new. But they had been in politics before." As a boy he had attended Métis conferences in Winnipeg with his father. "I think they had been ready a long time," he says of the people he met while forming the National Indian Brotherhood. "It was just a matter of getting the internal work together." That — and money.

The early days were filled with creative financing. Courchene recalls getting his first funds out of a government program aimed at helping farming communities: he claimed he was a communications arm for a community of farmers. Such funding escapades were not confined to national groups whose leaders had long been suspicious of Indian Affairs' largesse. The 1969 announcement of money to support political organizations was no exception. "When you get down to it," says Saul Terry, "it was still the department that had the say about how the funding would be appropriated. They still had accounting control." And they still do. Cardinal views Ottawa's funding approach even more cynically. He explains that, in the year before the White Paper policy, native leaders had effectively tapped non-Indian Affairs sources and were gaining, at least in the western provinces, a sense of autonomy. "Of course, whenever a bureaucrat gets frightened he gets very conscious of democracy," says Cardinal. "He wants to know who is representing these upstart groups and can they prove they represent these interests."

As well, explains Cardinal, the 25 cent per capita maximum allotted in the White Paper to the National Indian Brotherhood would effectively cut off other funding sources, a guarantee that the groups would have no voice. "We fought like hell to

make sure that funding through [other sources] continued."
According to Cardinal, the National Indian Brotherhood lost
the battle because Indian Affairs, faced with the political
vacuum left when the White Paper was withdrawn, transferred
responsibility for the groups over to the Secretary of State and
other federal bureaucracies. The move left Indians with the
same problem of funding restrictions that marked their relationship with Indian Affairs.

Money to maintain staff and programs conducted by Indian
political organizations and other native groups currently comes
from a variety of sources, primarily the Secretary of State for
core funding and the Canadian Employment and Immigration
Program. The Secretary of State began financing native organizations in 1971 under a program called the Aboriginal
Representative Organizations Program. In 1989, the budget for
that program stood at more than $11 million and was about to
become a major target of government budget restraints. Outside
of the Secretary of State, the various native political bodies are
not funded as political lobby groups. Other funds are granted
for specific programs and research that fall under the mandate
of various federal departments, such as Native Affairs and
Health and Welfare, and of provincial government departments. The organizations compete not only with other non-native groups for limited funds, but also with each other. One
Indian spokesperson says that using these various sources for
money is "like reinventing the wheel." Securing enough core
funding from Secretary of State is tough, and frequently organizations fall victim to government cuts and manipulation.
On top of that, the hiring and firing of staff is based on an
organization's ability to come up with a program that fits a
department's specific criteria but that offers little long-term
stability for the group.

During the 1970s, there emerged a new hybrid of native
political organization called the tribal council. Councils act as
umbrella groups which work on projects beneficial to a number
of bands in a particular geographic area. The original idea was
to have the tribal councils eventually take over the work
of Indian Affairs once the federal bureaucracy had been

dismantled — another White Paper proposal that appears to be dead.

As the Indian hierarchy became more complex, groups found themselves competing to stay alive. Saul Terry of the Union of British Columbia Indians describes how in 1983 he stopped going to the tribal council for money. As was proposed in the White Paper, the union was expected to tap into the council's money for part of its funding. But the competition for limited funds was detrimental to the native cause. "I told them this organization is not haggling over consultation funding. We don't want to fight with our own people over this." It was a particularly difficult decision for the union at the time.

The B.C. organization was one of ten provincial and five national aboriginal groups that became heavily involved between 1978-82 in Prime Minister Trudeau's dream to end Canada's role as a British colony. At the time, the country's native organizations had wound down from their united lobby effort against the White Paper and were dealing primarily with regional concerns. However, the repatriation of the Constitution offered them another opportunity to fight as a united front for their vision of being recognized as equal players within the federal framework. This time around, native leaders argued that their treaties were constitutional documents, and that if the original signatory — the Queen — was about to hand over the authority to a new party, then native people had a right to be at the table to ensure their rights would be protected and incorporated into any new deal.

According to several accounts of the aboriginal role in the constitutional debate, native Canadians came to the table with an unplanned and eventually expensive strategy to try for an equal place with the provincial leaders. Considering that the Federation of Saskatchewan Indians had only coined the term "Indian government" in 1977, native leaders had a long uphill battle and little time to explain to their own people and the rest of Canada what they envisioned their role should be. According to University of British Columbia law professor Douglas Sanders, whose detailed account of the native constitutional lobby effort has appeared in several publications, aboriginal groups began the debate with their three major organizations united behind two general demands: that their aboriginal and treaty rights be entrenched in the new Constitution, and that Indians be involved in the process of reform. This program would later be expanded to include recognition of aboriginal self-government, which would become a bone of contention among native groups and non-native power brokers.

Native people's initial efforts to be heard received only passing attention. Trudeau's response in the early rounds was an amendment which stated that nothing, even the equality provision of the Charter of Rights, would erase the special rights given to Indians in the Royal Proclamation of 1763. He also extended an invitation to three of the key native organizations — the National Indian Brotherhood, the Native Council of Canada (formerly the Canadian Métis Society), and the Inuit Committee on National Issues — to attend the October 1978 first ministers' meeting as observers. Another invitation was issued for the February 1979 first ministers' gathering. At the second meeting, with the Quebec referendum on the horizon and the need for support growing, Trudeau offered to add to the agenda a new item dealing with native issues in general terms. But the three groups rejected the overtures as too little and began to make other plans.

## Twelve Key Points

In June 1980, one month after the Quebec referendum on sovereignty-association was defeated, Trudeau's constitutional plan was accelerated. As *Globe and Mail* reporters Robert Sheppard and Michael Valpy describe in their account, *The National Deal*, two years of discussions and debate were reduced to twelve key points to be debated at a September meeting. All other outstanding issues were left for a "second round" of debate to take place after the Constitution was brought home. Aboriginal issues were not among the twelve points. Native Canadians were told again to wait. Trudeau argued that the delay was the result of a failure of native leaders to offer clear definitions of their goals. Native leaders were furious, but refused to bow out so early. Instead, they intensified their efforts. When the first ministers met in September, the National Indian Brotherhood held a parallel conference that brought hundreds of native people to Ottawa. The National Indian Brotherhood also began making plans to send a team to lobby the Queen and anyone else who would listen, from parliamentarians to human rights groups.

In October 1980, the National Indian Brotherhood opened an office in London. The Native Council of Canada took the fight for native people to have a say in the new Constitution to the international stage. There was an appearance in Amsterdam before the Bertrand Russell Peace Foundation in an international tribunal on human rights. The foundation declared the Canadian government guilty of "ethnocide" but the decision got little notice at home. In November, the Union of British Columbia Indians chartered a train called the *Constitutional Express*. More than 500 Indians made the trip to Ottawa to publicize their fight. And so the pressure mounted.

In January 1981, Jean Chrétien, then justice minister in charge of constitutional matters, introduced an amendment: "The aboriginal and treaty rights of the aboriginal peoples of Canada are hereby recognized and affirmed. In this act, aboriginal people of Canada include the Indian, Inuit and Métis." There was also notice that the Charter's equality provision did not negate special-status provisions for native people. Two days later, Chrétien introduced another amendment that would allow any province and Ottawa to opt out of the aboriginal rights clause. Faced with fierce opposition from native leaders, New Democrats and other sympathizers, he withdrew the offending clause almost immediately. But the die was cast.

While the provincial and federal leaders were obviously suffering from last-minute jitters about what the rights clause meant, it was the native groups who put the knife to the deal when their united front disappeared. Within days of the Chrétien offer, the fragile front began to disintegrate as various native groups across the country declared that the deal did not go far enough to guarantee their rights. Indian leaders viewed the use of the words "aboriginal rights" instead of "Indian rights" as another government attempt to diminish their status and treaty rights to the same level as the Métis, and to discredit a growing recognition of Indians as an easily identifiable and unified force. (The Métis are wards of the provincial governments and Indian leaders say the provinces have done a poor job of providing for them.) The National Indian Brotherhood considered the word "aboriginal" to be a diluted version of "Indian" and the government's way of undermining the growing strength and visibility of various Indian groups as they took their demands based on signed treaties to both the national and the international stages. "The tactic has always been that as long as you were dealing with identifiable, strongly visible Indian governments that say here are our treaties, then it was hard to deny the reality," says Cardinal, who along with several historians takes a dim view of Trudeau's earlier 1969 suggestion that the Métis should be brought into the aboriginal debate. Using the generic term "aboriginal" weakens the identifiable group, he says. "It is as if all of a sudden you have put a smoke screen in front of it. When you try and redefine it, then it becomes easier to mould the kind of answers you have been working for all along."

By April, the National Indian Brotherhood had withdrawn its support for the amendment while lobbying in England had hit some serious snags. British Columbia and Alberta natives had launched law suits in the British court asking for support of their position that the Crown was ultimately responsible for the treaties and that they had a legal right to be at the table for negotiation of repatriation of the Constitution. In January, the British House of Commons Foreign Affairs Committee concluded that treaty obligations had been transferred to Canadian jurisdiction under the 1931 Statute of Westminster. Such a decision is binding on the courts in England, and when the court decision came down, it reflected the committee's finding. The Indian lobby moved back to the British Parliament, but the fight was practically over.

On November 5, 1981, the results of an all-night session attended by Trudeau and nine provinces (Quebec was not included) were released. Aboriginal issues had disappeared.

These issues were reactivated by intense lobbying, including a vow by the New Democratic Party that it would vote against the resolution if changes were not made. A watered-down constitutional amendment that recognized "existing aboriginal and treaty rights" made it into the final package. While the final result was less than native organizations had fought for, the five-year battle gave native leaders across the country an opportunity to focus more clearly on what their goals were as a group and as separate bodies and to get the term "self-goverment" firmly placed in the national conscience. The lessons learned along the way, however, were expensive ones. It is estimated that Canada's native organizations spent $4.5 million fighting the constitutional battle. The Federation of Saskatchewan Indians alone travelled to London six times in a two-year period.

The first constitutional round was followed by a series of four first ministers' conferences on aboriginal rights. The last ended in 1987 with the ministers' refusal to entrench what they called "the undefined right of aboriginal self-government" in the Constitution. Since this failure to win full recognition in the constitutional process, native people have continued to seek their rights both in the Meech Lake agreement and on other fronts. There has been much to keep them busy.

In 1989, the Conservative government of Prime Minister Brian Mulroney showed that it was no different from previous governments when it came to undermining native goals and cutting funding. Alberta was the target this time, and the focus was the Lubicon Indian Band. The band has had a protracted land dispute with its own government and Ottawa, and has conducted an effective, embarrassing public relations campaign. Every tactic has been used, from blockades to keep oil companies off the land in 1988 to demonstrations at the Calgary Winter Olympics that same year. In an obvious attempt to undermine the Lubicon battle, the federal government agreed in July 1989 to sponsor a new Alberta band and create a new reserve. The second Lubicon band is made up of about twenty former Lubicon members who disagreed with the demands of Lubicon Chief Bernard Ominayak. They wanted him to accept

a government offer he had already rejected. The federal move
to support the splinter group flew directly in the face of what
has been a longstanding policy against recognizing any new
Indian bands in Canada.

In early 1990, as newspapers carried daily examples of vic-
tories for native people on a variety of fronts, the Mulroney
government delivered another series of blows at native organizations, particularly at the higher profile tribal councils and
the Assembly of First Nations. Three days after Finance Minister Michael Wilson delivered a cost-cutting budget, which
shifted much more financial responsibility onto the provinces,
twenty-eight political and cultural native organizations across
Canada were informed that after nineteen years their core funding from the Secretary of State was being cut. Within three
months, the twenty-eight groups would lose all their base funding and be forced to survive on the program money they used
to buttress their accounts. For many groups, this meant that
more than 50 per cent of their budgets had been wiped out;
seven other groups would see a reduction of 15 per cent. Total
cost-cutting to organizations amounted to $3.4 million.

Lobby groups were not the only target. In the same move,
the Secretary of State eliminated a $3.5 million native com-
munications program, which would seriously affect native-lan-
guage newspapers across the country and other native
television and radio initiatives. Georges Erasmus, national
chief of the Assembly of First Nations, was stunned by the
news. His organization was set to lose $562,000. "We're going
to try and convince this government they've made a tragic
mistake," he says. "It is extremely shortsighted and I think it's
suicidal." Other native leaders charged that the move against
their political bodies and communication arms was a direct
attack against their growing impact.

Ottawa has denied the charge, saying simply that all
Canadians had to tighten their belts and that only groups
believed to have some hope of finding other sources of funding,
mostly status Indian tribal councils, were hit. Métis and non-
status groups were informed that their budget would be cut by
only 7.5 per cent because they had nowhere else to go to ask

for money. Status Indians were being told to take hat in hand to Indian Affairs or their provincial governments and beg for already scarce funds.

Within hours of hearing the budget news, Erasmus was on the airwaves telling Canadians that the government had dealt native groups a devastating blow. He had facts, figures, and a way of putting them together that allowed people to visualize the impact. "The situation among indigenous people in this country is absolutely deplorable. We are the Third and Fourth World Canada," he said. "The government is trying to keep us from explaining to Canadians the actual situation we live in." The Mulroney government had cut per-capita spending on native people by 11 per cent since 1985-86, Erasmus charged. To meet the 1985-86 level of $4,658 spent on each of the 440,000 Indians in Canada, the government would have had to increase native spending by $333 million.

Erasmus, a Dene from the Northwest Territories, is typical of the native leader of the 1980s. A high school graduate, he got his leadership training in the late 1960s and 1970s at the grassroots level. He became heavily embroiled in the land claims negotiations of the Dene Nation (previously the Indian Brotherhood of the Northwest Territories) and fought the Mackenzie Valley Pipeline. He was elected vice-chief of the troubled Assembly in 1983 and national chief two years later. Like other native organizations which had lived through the recession of the early 1980s and the constitutional battle, the Assembly was in series debt (more than $3.5 million) and divided over its most recent election. But within three years, Erasmus had eliminated the debt and had brought everyone back under the same roof to fight the common opponent in Ottawa.

But it was in the debate over the Meech Lake Accord that Canada's native organizations were able to show just how much they had really grown. As in the repatriation debate, Canada's aboriginal people rejected the Meech Lake Accord because it ignored them and their right to be at the table to negotiate on their own behalf. The Meech Lake document would, among other things, entrench a vision of Canada recognizing Quebec as a distinct society and the French and English as the two founding nations. The role of Canada's first people was ignored. To quell their protests, the eleven first ministers borrowed a tactic from the 1982 campaign by offering aboriginal people conferences every three years to discuss their concerns. There was also a promise of a committee to study the idea of including aboriginal people and the multicultural mosaic as fundamental characteristics of Canada. It was not enough. On June 11, 1990, only twelve days before the deadline for ratifying the accord, a lone member of the Manitoba legislature stood and stopped the progress of debate by challenging procedural issues. Elijah Harper, a Cree Indian from northern Manitoba and the first native MLA in Manitoba, became the unexpected hero of more than 440,000 native people across the country. His role was a sign of how native organizations have matured and thrived.

Although some leaders say they are being forced to fight the same battles they did twenty years ago, their common voice is slowly capturing the attention of Canadians and the world. And it will not be easily silenced. The new generation of articulate and sophisticated leaders includes a growing number of native lawyers, entrepreneurs, and civil service graduates who represent various bands and provinces. They all speak about their overriding common goal of self-determination no matter where they sit on the intricate details.

Native people have long recognized that their small numbers have often left them at a disadvantage. But there is a growing sense of urgency, heightened by a demographic trend in the native population. According to the 1986 census, almost 61 per cent of the country's aboriginal population (Indian, Métis, and Inuit) is under the age of twenty-four, compared with 38 per cent of the Canadian population. The demands of this relatively young, frustrated, often angry group, with its education and keen awareness of native injustice, will become harder and harder to ignore. Throughout the debate on native issues, there have been repeated warnings of potential violence. To date, native people have turned this violence inward, destroying each other and themselves. In 1988 Erasmus delivered the warning again, and the dynamics of the youth movement have made several observers pause to take another look at the issue. "We say, Canada, deal with us today because our militant leaders are already born," Erasmus said in an Edmonton speech to the Assembly of First Nations.

Keith Penner, former Liberal MP and chairman of a 1983 parliamentary committee on self-government, still hears from Canadians who see the poverty-stricken native person on the streets and ask how these people could possibly run their own affairs. In response, he says that these white people have never come face-to-face with some of the country's leading native spokespeople. When he hears the doubt in some people's voices, he draws them another picture: "When the White Paper failed dismally, the decision was made to turn the problem over to the native leaders which, in turn, began the politicization of Indian people," he says. "Since 1969 the number of Indian politicians has grown, and I would say that most of them are as good, if not better than MPs and premiers. In fact, I'm the one who feels inferior when I meet the top Indian leaders in this country."

# Postscript

It was in October 1989 that fifteen-year-old Nona Pariseau first posed the question that would eventually be included in the introduction to *The First Canadians*: "What is it that these Indian people want, anyway?" That question began simply as part of her research for a high school history project on native issues. But Pariseau's curiosity soon took her beyond the classroom. Her question was followed by several more, all filled with the frustration and impatience other Canadians have voiced about the apparent failure of aboriginal people to pull themselves together and get on with life, just like the immigrants who have settled here.

But after six months of talking to native people and debating the issues that have occupied the minds and hearts of Canada's aboriginal people for more than 200 years, the Halifax-born Pariseau is confident she has found some of the answers. "Native people have been denied their basic human rights," Pariseau told a student audience called together to hear a debate on the pros and cons of native self-government. "With the granting of self-government, natives will be getting back not only their human rights, but also a portion of what they had before white men began destroying them and their culture."

Pariseau encountered many obstacles before reaching her conclusions. She was bombarded with the same questions she herself had posed only months before — questions asked by fellow students who suffered from the same ignorance about aboriginal history and the same negative attitudes about Canada's native people. "Kids asked me why Indians just couldn't go back to their own country, or why they wanted their own province. They said that after self-government, native people would just want to take over our country. They treat them like some communist state, like they are foreigners, and think that they are poaching off us."

Pariseau says that her experience has led her to conclude that racism was at the root of her initial evaluation of the native situation and of the comments classmates made during the public debates. "I was blown away," she explains, referring to the angry retorts that were tossed at her during the discussions. "I could not believe how prejudiced [the students] were. They still think that Indians are the bums on Main Street. But what they really need to see and do is to take a look at the reserves and to take a look at the fact that these people are human beings."

Looking back over her experience, she is straightforward and candid. "Yes, I was prejudiced, but I try not to be now. When I first came here, it was a lack of knowledge. But I think if everyone put aside their prejudice, they would come to the same conclusion … that native people need their freedom." And she has no doubts that the native leaders she met can run their own lives, and already do. "There will be mistakes, but so what? We've made mistakes many times, and no one talks about that."

Pariseau pauses a long time when asked if she thinks native people will win their battle for self-government. "I don't know," she says finally, now aware of the struggle Canada's aboriginal people have faced over the centuries. "Look at how much we have taken away already. We have taken everything from them."

Pariseau says she believes the strong native leaders and their communities will survive against all the odds, but others may not. And she says she can see that Indian people might lose everything in their endless power struggles with the federal government if Canadians remain apathetic and uninformed. Trying to get the native message across, she says, may be the toughest fight of all. "It's just so sad, because every generation has to learn it all, over and over again."

# Bibliography

## GENERAL

Canada. Department of Indian Affairs and Northern Development. *Indian Conditions, A Survey.* 1989.

Canada. Department of Indian Affairs and Northern Development. *Main Estimates, 1967-1988.*

Canada. Department of Regional and Industrial Expansion. *Native Economic Development Program, Evaluation Study.* Prepared by Haskins-Sills, Deloitte (consultants).

Canada. Department of Regional and Industrial Expansion. *Review of Native Economic Development Program (NEDP), Element 1, Final Report.* 24 Nov. 1988.

Canada. Report to Parliament. *Implementation of the 1985 Changes to the Indian Act.*

Canada. Statistics Canada. *1986 Census.*

Frideres, James. *Native People in Canada: Contemporary Conflicts.* Toronto: Prentice Hall, 1983.

MacGregor, Roy. *Chief, The Fearless Vision of Billy Diamond.* Toronto: Penguin Books, 1989.

York, Geoffrey. *The Dispossessed: Life and Death in Native Canada.* Toronto: Lester & Orpen Dennys, 1989.


## THE WHITE PAPER

Asch, Michael. *Home and Native Land: Aboriginal Rights and the Canadian Constitution.* Toronto: Methuen, 1984.

Canada. Department of Indian Affairs and Northern Development. *Statement of the Government of Canada on Indian Policy (The White Paper).* 1969.

Canada. A Study Team Report to the Task Force (Neilsen Task Force) on Program Review. *Improved Program Delivery, Indians and Natives.* 1985.

Indian Tribes of Manitoba. *Wahbung, Our Tomorrow.* 1971 (obtained from the Department of Indian Affairs and Northern Development.)

Sheppard, Robert and Valpy, Michael. *The National Deal, The Fight for the Canadian Constitution.* Toronto: Macmillan, 1982.

## RESERVES

Canada. Department of Indian and Northern Affairs. *Survey of Bill C-31 Applicants*. Prepared by Coopers & Lybrand Consulting Group. 10 June 1988.

Canada. *DIAND's Costing Methodology and Questions on Bill C-31, a series of methodology papers prepared for the Assembly of First Nations Chiefs Committee on Bill C-31*. Prepared by the office of John Rayner, assistant deputy minister of Indian services. Spring 1988.

Canada. Indian and Northern Affairs Canada. *Highlights of Aboriginal Conditions 1981-2001, Part I, Demographic Trends*. Working Paper Series 89-3. Prepared by N. Janet Hagey, Gilles Larocque, and Catherine McBride, Quantitative Analysis and Socio-demographic Research. Finance and Professional Services. October 1989.

Canada Mortgage and Housing Corporation. *Evaluation of CMHC On-Reserve Housing Programs and Summary Report*. Program Evaluation Division, Operations Review Directorate. May 1987.

Lithwick, N.H.; Schiff, Marvin; and Vernon, Eric. *An Overview of Registered Indian Conditions in Canada*. Lithwick Rothman Schiff Associates Ltd., for Indian and Northern Affairs Canada. 1986.

## URBAN INDIANS

Dosman, J. Edgar. *Indians, The Urban Dilemma*. Toronto: McClelland and Stewart, 1978.

Institute for Research on Public Policy. *Dynamics of Government Programs for Urban Indians in the Prairie Provinces*. 1984.

Krotz, Larry. *Urban Indians: The Strangers in Canada's Cities*.

Manitoba, Northern Affairs Department. *Workshop on the Development of an Indian and Metis Urban Strategy in Manitoba*. 1989.

Ryan, Joan. *Wall of Words: The Betrayal of the Urban Indian*. Calgary: University of Calgary, Department of Anthropology, 1978.

Urban Indian Association of Manitoba. *Economic Strategy for Urban Indians*. 1987.

## SELF-GOVERNMENT

Angus Reid Poll. *Aboriginal Justice Issues*. 14 October 1989.

Canada. House of Commons Special Committee of Indian Self-Government. *Second Report*. 20 October 1983.

Cassidy, Frank and Bish, Robert L. *Indian Government: Its Meaning and Practice*. Oolichan Books and Institute for Research on Public Policy, 1989.

Franks, C.E.S. *Public Administration Questions Relating to Aboriginal Self-Government, Background Paper Number 12*. Kingston: Queen's University, Institute of Intergovernmental Relations, 1987.

## ECONOMIC DEVELOPMENT

Canada. House of Commons Special Committee on Self-Government. *The Economic Foundation of Indian Self-Government*. Prepared by Thalassa Research Associates, Victoria, B.C. 31 May 1983.

Canada. Department of Industry Science and Technology, and Manitoba Department of Northern Affairs. *Evaluation of the Canada/Manitoba Northern Development Agreement, Volume 1: Evaluations and Recommendations*. Prepared by Agreement Advisory Committee to the Canada/Manitoba Northern Development Agreement. December 1988.

Canada. Department of Industry, Science and Technology. *Executive Summary: Mid-Term Review of the Canada-Saskatchewan Northern Economic Development Subsidiary Agreement*. Prepared by Gail D. Surkan (consultant). n.d.

Canada. Department of Regional Economic Expansion. *An Evaluation of the Canada-Saskatchewan Interim Subsidiary Agreement on the Saskatchewan Northlands*. n.d.

Canada. Department of Regional Economic Expansion, and Alberta Department of Tourism and Small Business, Northern Development Branch. *Canada-Alberta North Subsidiary Agreement Assessment*. Prepared by Co-West Associates, Edmonton, Alberta. 15 October 1980.

Canada. Department of Regional Economic Expansion. *Canada/Saskatchewan Northlands Agreement Evaluation: Future Directions for Cost-Shared Programs in Northern Saskatchewan*. Prepared by DPA Consulting Limited, Bell, Ahenakew & Associates, Damas & Smith. December 1982.

Hawthorn, H.B., ed. *A Survey of The Contemporary Indians of Canada: A Report on Economic, Political, Education Needs and Policies*. Two Volumes. Indian Affairs Branch. October 1966.

Canada. Department of Regional Economic Expansion. *Canada/Saskatchewan Northlands Agreement Evaluation: Main Report*.

Prepared by DPA Consulting Limited, Bell, Ahenakew & Associates, Damas & Smith. December 1982.

## HEALTH CARE

Canada. Health and Welfare Canada. *Annual Reports, Medical Services Branch, Manitoba Region and National, 1967-1987.*

Canada. Health and Welfare Canada. *Suicide in Canada. Report from the Task Force on Suicide in Canada.* 1987.

Canada. Health and Welfare Canada. *Vital Statistics.* Prepared by the Planning and Evaluation Unit, Manitoba Region, Medical Services Branch. 1986.

Canada. Department of Indian Affairs and Northern Development. *Indian Conditions, A Survey.* 1989.

Lithwick, N.H.; Schiff, Marvin; and Vernon, Eric. *An Overview of Registered Indian Conditions in Canada.* Lithwick Rothman Schiff Associates Ltd., for Indian and Northern Affairs Canada. 1986.

## EDUCATION

Assembly of First Nations. *Tradition and Education: Towards A Vision of Our Future, National Review of First Nations Education, volumes 1 and 3.* Ottawa: April 1988.

Canada. Department of Indian Affairs and Northern Development. *Indian Education Paper, Phase 1.* 1 May 1982.

Canada. Indian and Northern Affairs Canada. *Basic Departmental Data.* Evaluation directorate. July 1988.

Canada. Indian and Northern Affairs Canada. *Education of Indians in Federal and Provincial Schools in Manitoba, Evaluation Report.* 31 August 1978.

Canada. Indian and Northern Affairs Canada. *Highlights of Aboriginal Conditions 1981-2001, Part III, Economic Conditions.* Working Paper Series 89-3. Prepared by N. Janet Hagey, Gilles Larocque, and Catherine McBride, Quantitative Analysis and Socio-demographic Research. Finance and Professional Services. October 1989.

Canada. Indian and Northern Affairs Canada. *Post-Secondary Education Assistance Evaluation Study, Final Report.* Prepared by DPA Group Inc. for the Evaluation Branch, Corporate Policy, INAC. January 1985.

Canada. *Main Estimates, 1967/68* through to *1988/90.*

Canada. Statistics Canada. *1986 Census — Characteristics of Ethnic Groups, Showing Single and Multiple Origins by Sex, for Canada.* 1988.

Chrétien, Jean. *A Venture in Indian Education* (speech). Address to Council of Ministers of Education. Regina, Saskatchewan. 23 June 1972. (Department of Indian Affairs and Northern Development.)

Manitoba, Department of Community Services. *No Quiet Place. Review Committee on Indian and Métis Adoptions and Placements, Final Report.* Associate Chief Judge Edwin C. Kimelman, chairman. 1985.

## CHILD WELFARE

Canada. Department of Indian Affairs and Northern Development. *An Assessment of Services Delivered Under the Canada-Manitoba-Indian Child Welfare Agreement.* Coopers and Lybrand Consulting Group. 27 August 1987.

Canada. Department of Indian Affairs and Northern Development. *Indian Child and Family Services Management Regime, Discussion Paper.* October 1989.

Canada. Indian and Northern Affairs Canada and Family Services Task Force. *Indian Child and Family Services in Canada. Final Report.* 1987.

Canada. House of Commons Special Committee of Indian Self-Government. *Second Report.* Ottawa: Queen's Printer for Canada. 20 October 1983.

Johnston, Patrick. *Native Children and the Child Welfare System.* Toronto: Canadian Council on Social Development, 1983.

Manitoba. Department of Community Services. *No Quiet Place. Review Committee on Indian and Métis Adoptions and Placements, Final Report.* Associate Chief Judge Edwin C. Kimelman, chairman. 1985.

## JUSTICE

Canada. Solicitor General of Canada. *Correctional Issues Affecting Native People.* Correctional Law Review Working Paper. 1988.

Canada. Solicitor General of Canada. *Native People and Justice Report on the National Conference and the Federal/Provincial Conference on Native Peoples and the Criminal Justice System.* February 1975.

Canada. Solicitor General of Canada. *Native Policing in Canada: A Review of Current Issues.* 1986.

Canadian Bar Association. *Report of the Canadian Bar Association Committee on Aboriginal Rights in Canada: An Agenda for Action.* 1988.

Jackson, Michael. *Locking up Natives in Canada.* A report for the Canadian Bar Association Committee, Imprisonment and Release. 1988.

Morse, Bradford and Lock, Linda. *Native Inmates in Provincial and Federal Institutions.* For the Canadian Sentencing Commission's Native Inmate Project. 1985.

Simon Fraser University. *Conference on Northern Justice.* 1973.

Sinclair, Murray. *Closing Remarks for the Manitoba Aboriginal Justice Inquiry (Part One).* 28 April 1989.

Social Policy Research Associates. *National Evaluation Overview of Indian Policing.* July 1983.

Stevens, Samuel. *Access to Civil Justice for Aboriginal Peoples.* Conference on Access to Civil Justice, University of British Columbia. June 1988.

# Index